THE PRODIGIES OF EGYPT

THE PRODIGIES OF EGYPT

Treating of the PYRAMIDS,

The Inundation of the *Nile,* and other PRODIGIES of EGYPT,
According to the *Opinions* and *Traditions* of the ARABIANS.

Written Originally in the *Arabian* Tongue by
Murtadi the Son of *Gaphiphus*.

Rendered into *French* by Monsieur *Vattier,*
Arabick Professor to the King of *France.*

And thence faithfully done into *English* by J. DAVIES of *Kidwelly.*

JasonColavito.com Books
ALBANY, NY · 2015

BIBLIOGRAPHIC NOTE

This edition, first published in 2015, is an unabridged republication of *The Egyptian History* translated by J. Davies and printed by R. Battersby for Thomas Bassett in London in 1672.

Introduction and translation of sections of the *Akhbār al-zamān* copyright © 2015 Jason Colavito. All rights reserved.

All Rights Reserved. No part of this book may be reproduced or transmitted by any means, electronic or mechanical, including photocopy, recording, or any other information storage and retrieval system, in any form whatsoever (except for copying permitted by U.S. copyright law or by reviewers for the public press), without the express written permission of the author.

Published by Jason Colavito, Albany, New York

This book has been newly typeset for this edition in Charis SIL

ISBN-13: 978-1515177951
ISBN-10: 1515177955

www.JasonColavito.com

A Note on the Text

Abū l-Ḥassan Murtaḍā b. al-'Afīf Abī l-Ǧawd Ḥātim b. al-Musallam b. Abī l-'Arab al Ḥāriṯī al Maqdisī, better known as Murtaḍā ibn al-'Afīf or Murtadi, son of Gaphiphus, was an obscure Arabian writer born in 1154 or 1155 CE.[*] His family was originally from the area near Jerusalem, and he studied in Alexandria, Damascus, and Cairo. He received brief notice in the works of his contemporaries, as well as several later authors, but while he is credited with having written many books, no titles survive, not even the original title of his only complete work to survive to modern times, the book known variously as the *Egyptian History* or the *Prodigies of Egypt*, which reported traditional folklore associated with the pyramids, the Flood, and the wonders of Egypt. Murtaḍā ibn al-'Afīf died in Cairo on June 25, 1237, but his *Egyptian History* long outlived him.

A copy of his book made in 1584 ended up in the library of Cardinal Mazarin, the Bibliothèque Mazarine, where the French polymath Pierre Vattier (1623-1667) found it and translated it into French while residing in Montreuil in Normandy in 1665. Unfortunately, the original Arabic was lost, leaving this French edition, published in 1666 as *L'Égypte de Murtadi, fils du Gaphiphe*, as the surviving text of Murtaḍā's work. This translation, in turn, was rendered into English in 1672 by the onetime Republican John Davies (1625-1693), and this translation is reproduced here. Davies's translation, published as *The Egyptian History* but with internal headings labeling it *The Prodigies of Egypt*, found favor with reform-minded figures and played a role in English interest in alchemical, Hermetic, and heretical

---

[*] Biographical information herein is taken from Yūsuf Rāġib, "L'auteur de *L'Égypte de Murtadi fils du Gaphiphe*," *Arabica* 21, no. 2 (June 1974): 203-209.

materials. Passages from the book, likely in its French version, went on to inspire Clara Reeves's Gothic novella *The History of Charoba* (1785) and through it W. S. Landor's Romantic epic poem *Gebir* (1798). That poem, in turn, inspired Samuel Taylor Coleridge, Percy Bysshe Shelley, Walter Scott, and other Romantics, with Shelley so enamored of it that a friend once threw the book out the window to stop his ceaseless reading.

While this edition endeavors to preserve the first English translation's text as much as possible, it differs from Davies's original publication in a few respects. First, the old printing of Davies used for this text contained some sections that were illegible or damaged. For the most part, the missing letters or words were easily restored; in a few cases, I have provided missing text by translating from Vattier's French edition. Second, I have added quotation marks to help clarify when the author is quoting another source, or when characters are speaking. In some cases, this is not always entirely clear, and the quotation marks are only a rough guide to distinctions the French and English translators did not specify. In a few cases I have amended archaic spellings, but only when the older spelling would have made it impossible to understand the meaning of the sentence. Finally, I have amended some references to the prophet Muhammad where changes in the English language have rendered the original references culturally insensitive. For example, Vattier's French translation, repeated by Davies, renders the epithet "the unlettered prophet" (Quran 7:158) as "*prophète-idiot*," from the older meaning of "idiot" as "ignorant" or "uneducated." Due to the changes in the connotation of the word, I have restored the more correct Quranic reading to avoid misunderstandings.

To this text I have appended parallel passages on the pyramids from the *Akhbar al-zamān* of pseudo-Mas'ūdī, written sometime between 904 and 1140 and useful as a comparison between Murtaḍā's version of antediluvian history and other traditional accounts. This account I have translated from the French edition published as *L'abrégé des Merveilles* by the Baron Carra de Vaux in 1898.

To my Honoured Uncle, Mr. JOHN GRIFFITH
Of *Llangwendraeth* in the County of *Carmarthen*.

Dear Uncle,

When I was upon the Translation of this Piece, I often entertained you with several *Stories* of it, and you thought them not unpleasant. You now have them all together; and what must needs add to your satisfaction and diversion, you will find a strange account (according to the *Arabians*) of a Countrey, which affords matter of Admiration to those who travel thither even in our days. You know how often I have bemoan'd your loss of divers excellent *Manuscripts, Prophecies, Poetry,* and other Subjects, relating to our own Countrey; for certainly nothing so pleasant as to survey the Genius and Humours of our earliest Predecessors. But since it is vain to call Time to an account for all the excellent things it hath devoured, and to fasten on its *Envy* what is justly attributed to Humane *Negligence,* give me leave to recommend this *Prodigious* Treatise (which hath had the Fortune to escape its Teeth) to your perusal; and when I consider, with what complacency you quote and reflect on the *Actions* and *Apophthegmes* of those who have Inhabited the World many *Centuries* of years before us, I cannot doubt but you will approve the publick acknowledgment I make, by the present address, of my being,

Honour'd Uncle, Your most affectionate Nephew, and humble Servant,
J. DAVIES.

A TABLE of the most remarkable things
in the ensuing HISTORY OF *EGYPT*.

The French author's preface rendered into English. vii

PART ONE

The Priests of *Egypt*. 2
The *Cater*. 3
The Magick of the *Egyptian* Priests. 4
Gancam King and Priest commands Spirits to build him a Palace. 4
The Priestess *Borsa*, and her *Acts*. 5
The Brazen Tree. 7
The Maritime Pyramid. 8
Divers Kings of *Egypt*. 9
The City of the *Black Eagle*. 10
The Pyramids built by *Aclimon*. 11
Saurid's Mirrour. 13
Pyramids built before the Deluge. 14
The Brothers Annals. 15
The three Pyramids. 16
The Guards of the Pyramids. 19
Stories of the Pyramids, I, II, III, IV, V. 20.
Predictions made to King *Saurid*. 24
Nebuchodonozor. 25
The Spirits of the Pyramids. 26
History of the Deluge. 28
King *Darmasel*. 30
The Ark. 34
The Deluge. 35
Different opinions of the Deluge. 36
The History of *Noah*, according to an Ancient Book found by the Author. 37

Noah's Wife. 39
The time from *Adam* to the Deluge. 41
The Elephant and Lion in the Ark. 41
What part the Devil hath in the Vine. 42
The Scorpion and the Serpent. 43
Kings of *Egypt* before the Deluge. 44
Darmasel and *Philemon*. 44
Moncatam's Chemistry. 48
The *Pharaos* of *Alexandria*. 49
Noah's Prayer for *Masar*. 49
Masar's Tomb. 51
Kings of *Egypt* after the Deluge. 51
The History of *Abraham* and *Totis* King of *Egypt*. 52
Charoba, *Totis*'s Daughter. 53
Abraham's Prayer for *Charoba*. 54
Charoba poisoning her Father reigns after him. 56
The History of *Gebirus* and *Charoba*. 57
The Nymph *Marina*. 59
Painters in the bottom of the Sea. 60
The seven Tombs. 61
Charoba's Nurse defeats *Gebirus* and his Army. 63
Charoba's death. 65
Dalica Queen of *Egypt*. 65
Kings of *Egypt* after her. 65

PART TWO

Words of *Mahumet* advantageous to *Egypt.* 67
Augmentation of the *Nile.* 68
A Virgin Sacrific'd to that end. 69
Pharao. 71
Sources of the *Nile.* 72
Causes of its overflowing. 73
Qualities of *Egypt.* 76
The History of the *Egyptian* Slave. 77
Other qualities of *Egypt.* 79
Gamra and *Zephta.* 83
Omar. 84
The Land of *Alphiom.* 85
The *Mamunus.* 85
The *Rajan, Joseph's Pharao.* 87
The Acts of *Joseph* in *Egypt.* 89
A second story of *Alphiom.* 89
The *Nilometer.* 90
A third story of *Alphiom.* 91
A fourth story of it. 93
Joseph's Prison. 93
The place of *Jacob's* Camel. 95
Zelicha, Joseph's Mistress. 95
Caphor's Prayer. 96
Joseph's Prayer. 97
The Pyramids. 98
Macherir the Blind man. 99
Mussulman Daemons. 101
The Pyramids. 102
Quisias the son of *Caltham.* 103
The Front of a Mosquey. 105
The augmentations of the Mosquey of *Masre.* 108
History read in the Mosquey. 110
The green Tables of the Mosquey of *Masre.* 110
Pharao's Castle. 112
Caron the Wealthy, who is *Corah.* 113
Moses's Chemistry. 114
Omars Letter to *Gamrou.* 117
Gamrou's answer to *Omar.* 118
A supposed Statue of *Mahumet* at *Masre.* 121
Another alleged Statue of *Mahumet.* 122
Mary of *Egypt.* 123
The last words of *Mahumet.* 124
Other words of *Mahumet.* 125
The words of a Sage of *Egypt.* 125
The Prophets and devout Persons liv'd by their Labour. 126
The cries of a Devote at the Mosquey Gate of *Masre:* 126

Appendix: An Early Arabic Account of Pyramid Legends 129

The French Author's Preface *Rendred into English,* Giving an account of the design of this Treatise, and its publishing.

E*gypt* is a Province so pregnant in prodigies, that, from the earliest times, those, whose curiosity excited them to the knowledge of excellent things, have made it one of the principal objects of their considerations. *Pliny* names thirteen famous Authors, who had written before him of the *Pyramids,* which are one of the things admir'd therein; and *Herodotus* desirous to say something of that Countrey in general, before he came to the particular Narration of the expedition which *Cambyses* King of *Persia* had made into it, and whereto the design of his History led him, spent in that digression all his *Euterpe,* that is to say, one of the nine Books, wherein it was his intention to comprehend whatever had been remarkable in the World to this time. All the Authors who have since written in *Greek* or *Latine,* or any other Language known in *Europe,* have not omitted treating of the same subjects, according to the occasions they have had to do it, as being likely to prove the noblest Ornaments of their Works.

As concerning the *Arabians,* though the Treatise whereof I here publish the Translation be short enough, yet have they discoursed very amply of it in several Books: and it is not long since I saw in the Lord Chancellors Library two Manuscripts in Folio of great bulk, and close written, which treat only of the rarities and singularities of *Egypt;* at least, if the Titles, which have been put thereto, by such as have examined them, be true; for I have not yet had the opportunity to consider them at leisure. And therefore I shall not give any punctual account of them, calling to mind that at the beginning of this very Manuscript, out of which I have made this Translation, some Italian had written these words as it were for its Title, *De Negromanzia, e dell' origine di i Negromanti;* which had obliged me at first to slight it, and diverted me from looking more narrowly into it, if the beauty of the Original, and the Gold glittering in the two first pages, after the manner of other Books cuiously written in the *East,* had not engaged my longer consideration of them, whereby I was satisfied, that the *Italian* Inscription was not answerable to the *Arabian* Art, and could not forbear crying out, O *soeculum infelix!* as *Erasmus* did upon a like occasion, having found, as he saith, Commentaries on *Mimus Publianus; Qui neque coelum; neque erm attingerent, & tamen accuratissime depictos, ceu rem sacram.* This impertinent title had no doubt been given our Manuscript by a person who had casually cast his eye on some passages, where it mentions the Enchanters of *Egypt;* and the same injury might haply have be done, by a like precipitation, to the Sacred Books of *Genesis* and *Exodus,* wherein there is also mention made of those Magicians, and the wonderful effects of their Magick, which they had the impudence to compare with the Divine miracles of *Moses* and *Aaron.* These Enchanters then are part of the subject of this Book, but not all, as being one of the things, which many ages since had raised admiration in those who considered *Egypt,* but not the onely one, nor the principal in a Country, where the Earth, the Waters, and the Air out-vy one the other, in affording extraordinary subjects of Meditation to Philosophers upon natural things, and whose Inhabitants have signalized themselves by their prodigious structures, and by the invention even of Philosophy it self.

The Land of *Egypt* is it self a stranger in the place of its situation, if we credit the conjectures of it of Philosophers, who have attentively viewed and considered it; it came thither from a Countrey so remote, that the industry of men could never settle any Commerce for the importation of fruits from those places, whence nature conveys them the very soil whereby they are produced. The air there is in a perpetual serenity, never disturbed at any Season of the Year with Snow, Hail, Rain, Lightning, or Thunder. The Waters there rise to a prodigious height during the greatest heats of Summer, when they are elsewhere lowest, or dryed up; and in Winter, when they are every where either frozen up, or over-flown, they there gid gently below their ordinary course. The surface of the Earth is spread with a pleasant verdure, with so sweet a temperature of the Air, that the fairest Springs of other Countries come not near it. In the Moneth of *March,* the Harvest ready to be cut down, guilds the pregnant Fields, which are devested thereof before the Moneth of *April.* And in the Moneths of *July* and *August* the same Fields are changed into so many Seas, and the Cities and Villages into so many Islands, by a fortunate inundation, which spares the Inhabitants the trouble of tilling and manuring them, as must of necessity be done elsewhere; for the *Egyptians* have no more to do but to Sow the Seeds therein, when the Waters are fallen away, and slightly to stir the slime which is spread thereon, that they may be covered, which they did heretofore, as *Herodotus* relates by driving Herds of Swine after the Sowers. Thus do they get the Fruits of the most fertile piece of earth in the Universe, to use the terms of the same Author, most easily, and without any trouble; after they have gathered the productions of the Waters, by a yet more easie fishing, or rather as *Aelian* expresses it, by an Harvest of Fish, which lie scattered on the slime in the midst of the Fields.

These natural prodigies have alwaies engaged the greatest wits in an enquiry into their causes, which are reducible onely to two heads. For the serenity of the Air proceeds no doubt from the nature of the adjacent and neighbouring Countries and Waters, which are not apt to send thither any vapours, which might be condensed into Rain, Hail, or Snow; nor yet any mineral exhalations, which might cause thunder and lightning: and the other Miracles, which are seen by the Raies of that delightful Sun, are the effects of that admirable River, which keeps the Inhabitants of that Countrey in such quiet, after it hath brought them the soil which is to sustain and nourish them.

For the better understanding of this, it is to be observed that *Aegypt* is only a Plain, or rather a spacious Valley, reaching in length from *South* to *North* from the *Tropick* of *Cancer,* or a little beyond it, to the *Mediterranean* Sea, for the space of about two hundred and thirty Leagues; and in breadth, from *East* to *West,* between two Mountains, which are its limits, one towards *Arabia,* and the other towards *Africk,* but not alwaies at an equal distance one from the other. For at the Northern extremity, along the Shore of the *Mediterranean* Sea, that distance is about six score leagues; above the places where *Heliopolis* heretofore stood, and where now *Cairo* is, about fifty leagues distant from the Sea, it diminishes so for the space of about seventy leagues, that the two Mountains are not above six or seven leagues distant one from the other. Above that space they dilate again, and the Countrey grows wider, even to its Meridional extremitie, which makes the upper *Aegypt,* otherwise called *Thebais.* Thus is *Aegypt* naturally divided into three parts, which may be called *Upper,* the *Lower,* and the *Middle.* In the *Middle,* which is much narrower then the others, and which our Author calls *Gize,* as much as to say the *passage* was the City of *Memphis,* near the Western Mountain, on which not far thence there are several Pyramids, and those of the most sumptuous. In the *upper Aegypt* was heretofore the famous City *Thebes,* which had a hundred Gates, and was afterwards called *Diospolis;* and *Syene* seated directly under the Tropick of *Cancer;* so that the day of the Summer Solstice the Sun at noon shined to the bottoms of Wells, and streight and perpendicular Pillars made not any shade; and *Elephantina,* beyond which presently began *Ethiopia;* and *Copta,* whence there was a way to the Red Sea, the shortest and easiest of any along that Coast, by which there were brought on Camels abundance of *Indian* Commodities, which were afterwards embarqu'd on the *Nile;* and the little *Cataract,* where *Strabo* saies the Mariners fell down from the top to the bottom with their Boats, in the presence of the Governour of *Aegypt,* to make him sport; and the Lake of *Maeris,* with two Pyramids in the midst of it, each six hundred foot in height, three hundred under water, and three hundred above; and the *Labyrinth* yet more prodigious then the Pyramids. In the *Lower Aegypt* are the mouths of the *Nile,* whereof the two most distant one from the other make the *Delta,* which is a Triangular Island, the *Basis* whereof is the shore of the *Mediterranean* Sea, and the two sides the two arms of the *Nile,* which come to those mouths. *Cairo* is above the *Delta,* towards *Arabia,* near the place where heretofore *Heliopolis* stood. The *Arabians* now call it *Masre,* a name common to all *Aegypt,* and which we have several times rendred the *ancient Metropolis of Aegypt,* in the *Ma-*

humetan History. Alexandria is on the Sea-side near the Western mouth. The *Nile* flows in one single Chanel through the midst of the plain, from *Eliphantina* to the point of the *Delta,* which is about fifty leagues from the Sea; there it is divided into two, afterwards into several branches, before it falls into it.

Their conjecture, who held *Aegypt* to be a new Land, and come from some remote part, was that heretofore the space between the two Mountains from *Elephantina,* or a little below it, to *Alexandria* had been a gulph of the Sea, like, and in a manner parallel in its situation to that which is called the Red Sea, and entred into the Countries from the *North* towards the *South,* as the Red Sea enters into them from *South* to *North;* and that in processe of time the abundance of slime, which the *Nile* brings down when it is overflown, had filled that space, and framed therein the land which is now seen there, and which had no resemblance to those of *Arabia* and *Africk,* which are adjoyning thereto; whence they imagined it a stranger, and come from far. *Herodotus* was of opinion, that that collection of slime might have been made in less then twenty thousand years; taking haply his conjecture according to the increase of it from *Homer's* time to his own. For *Homer* affirms, that the Island of *Pharos* was in his time at a far greater distance from the Continent then it hath been since, as *Pliny* hath observed; inferring consequently thence, that *Aegypt* was augmented and advanced nearer the Sea.

What I think miraculous in this, is, that the Inhabitants of a Countrey which in appearance began not till a long time after the rest, should count the Years of their Antiquities in a far greater number then other Nations their Neighbours, and should make in their Countrey sumptuous Structures, which yet could not preserve the memorie of their Authors to a time, when other Nations were but in a manner beginning to entertain thoughts of doing somewhat of that kind, though they have lasted a long time after the ruine of those which were made much later. And yet all this methinks depends on the same cause, which is the excellency of the soil of that Province, and the facility of cultivating it; in as much as having always been able to maintain a far greater number of men then were requisite about the culture of it, the Princes, who were possessed thereof, were obliged to find out other employments for the greatest part of their Subjects; and this occasioned the early invention of *Philosophy* by those who were inclined to meditate on the wonderful things of nature, and to spend the rest allowed their bodies in employing the intellectual faculties of their souls in those noble labours. *Aristotle* speaks thus of it, when he says that they studyed Philosophy in *Aegypt* sooner then any where else, because there they soonest permitted the Priests to live in a commendable exemption from labour. As for others, who could only work with their hands, in regard the mild temperature of the Air dispenced with their employing themselves in many professions necessary elsewhere, to secure mens bodies from its injuries, it was requisite they should be employed in such works as might declare the powerfulness and magnificence of their Kings. Whence I conceive *Pliny* justly blameable for the character he gives these Miracles of the World, when he says they are *Regum pecuniae stulta ostentatio;* and that after he had said that those who had written of them before him differed about the Names of the Kings who built them, he should add these words, *Justissimo casu obliteratis tantae vanitatis authoribus.* For if all the works which contribute nothing to the supply of the necessities of humane life are follies. *Pliny* himself is in hazard to be esteemed to have done many; and this conceit of his is in my judgement much different from that of *Pythagoras,* who (as *Cicero* relates) affirms, that among the several sorts of persons who met ordinarily at the great general Assembly of all *Greece,* those who came not thither upon any business, nor out of design to get any thing, but only to see what passed, were the honester people; *Genus vel maxime ingenuum:* whom he therefore compared to the Philosophers.

These great Princes therefore are methinks rather to be bemoaned, that their Names were already forgotten above fifteen hundred years since, after they had made for the eternization thereof the Works which are to this day seen and admired, rather then they are to be blamed for having done such noble things. And this oblivion also no doubt proceeds from the excellency of their Countrey, which having been envyed by all Foreiners who have known it, hath always been one of the first preys of the Conquerours, and by that means so often changed Masters, that it is no wonder the memorie of the most Ancient should be lost; whereas the Princes, who once settled themselves therein, were well satisfied with that possession, and thought not of disturbing their Neighbours. True it is, that *Strabo* affirms, that in *Thebais* above *Diospolis,* and *Memnon*'s Temple, he saw on the magnificent Tombs of forty Kings, Obelisks, on which there were writings graven, which mentioned great Conquests made by those Kings, as far as *Scythia, Bactriana,* and the *Indies. Herodotus* affirms the same of *Sesstris;* but it may be doubted whether these great Conquerours were natural *Egyptians* or *Strangers,* who among other Countries had subdued *Aegypt;* for *Alexander* the Great was no *Aegyptian,* though he had his Tomb at *Alexandria,* and had been the Founder of that great City.

However it were yet this is certain, that the inclination of the Kings of *Aegypt* for great Structures is very ancient, since the *Pharao's* who Reigned in the times of *Joseph* and *Moses,* and who probably are comprehended by *Herodotus* under the single name of *Pheron,* had it, as may be seen by the complaints of the *Israelites* against them, when they made them work hard in the making of Brick, and paid them ill. That *Pheron* of *Herodotus* was such a Person as the *Pharao's* are represented to us; for he was no Conquerour, but an insolent and impious Prince, and the *Pharao's* were such as the *Arabian* expression at this day affirms it, who say, *To play the Pharao;* that is, to demean himself insolently and tyrannically: whence haply comes the *French* word, *Faire le Fanfaron.*

As to the Antiquity of the Sciences in *Aegypt* there is no doubt to be made of it, since *Plato* and *Eudoxus* learn'd Astronomy there in a School, where they studied thirteen years, and which was shewed at *Heliopolis* as a rarity in *Strabo*'s time, who affirms he saw it there; and adds, that the *Grecians* never knew exactly of how many Days, Hours, and Minutes the Year consisted, till they had read thereupon the Books of the Priests of *Aegypt,* which to that end were translated out of the *Aegyptian* Tongue into the *Greek;* which argues (by the way) that even at that time there were *Greek*

Versions made of Books writ in other Languages, contrary to the opinion which some Learned Men seem to have lately taken up.

That ancient Language of the *Aegyptians* was written from the right hand to the left, after the manner of the *Oriental* Tongues, as *Herodotus* hath observed: wherefore the *Coptick* writing now used from the left to the right seems rather to have come from the *Greek*, then the *Greek* from it, whatever *J. Kircher* tells us of it, in his *Prodromus Copticus*. As to the ancient Religion of the *Aegyptians,* though the Book we here Translate in several places mentions their Idols, *Strabo* affirms, that in his time there was not any Figure in their Temples, at least any representing a Man's body: whence it might be suspected that our Author took the Images of *Christian* Churches for Idols, since it may be particularly observed, that he seems in some places to put the Crosses into the same rank; which be it said without derogation from the approved Worship due to both. The same *Strabo,* (and before him *Herodotus)* would make us believe that *Circumcision,* and what they call *Excision,* which is the circumcision of Women, were ever used in *Aegypt,* and that the other Nations who observed it, as the *Colchi,*the *Ethiopians,* the *Phoenicians,* the *Syrians,* nay the *Jews* themselves took it from them; which is not without some ground; For Circumcision was not enjoyned *Abraham* till after his travelling into *Aegypt.* Strabo observes it as a singularity, that the *Aegyptians* brought up all the children that were born to them, which was not done by the *Greeks,* who exposed some, nay sometimes killed some of them, as we have it from *Terence* in his *Heautontimorumenos.* This commendable and indulgent custom, no doubt proceeded also from the goodness and fertility of their Countrey, which was such, that the children were no great charge to their Parents, and which endowed its Inhabitants with greater mildnesse of disposition, and tendernesse towards such as were so nearly related to them, then the *Greeks* had upon the like occasions.

The same Authors relate divers other remarkable things of the ancient Religion of *Aegypt,* and the manners of its inhabitants; all which have met with several changes by the Conquests which have been made of that Province at several times, since that at the very first, which is come to our knowledge, to wit, that of the *Persians,* 'tis questionlesse the Ceremonies of their Superstitions were very much altered by the persecution of *Cambyses,* which came to that height as to kill *Oxe Apis,* which passed for a God at *Memphis,* as some other Creatures did elsewhere; though all those which were reverenced by the *Aegyptians* in several places, were not adored in the quality of *Gods,* but many of them only in the quality of *Sacred Animals,* whom it was not lawful to injure. And it is very probable, according to *Cicero*'s conjecture, that at first they were all accounted only such, in asmuch as those who then governed the People thought fit for some reasons to preserve such Beasts as much as might be, as being advantageous for something; and that in processe of time the Superstition and Ignorance of those who comprehended not the true cause why they were spared, came to imagine something Divine in them; which in my judgment proceeded from the demeanour of the Priests towards other men, whom they blinded what they could, especially seeing the Priesthood belonged to certain Families, and was not communicable to all, no more then the other principal Functions of the Commonwealth, as Arms, Arts, and Agriculture; for that made every one absolutely ignorant of those things which belong'd not to him, and whereto he never had any right to aspire; and occasioned their being many times exercised by such as had not any natural disposition thereto, and consequently were not much capable thereof.

This Mysterious Carriage of the *Egyptian* Priests extended not onely to things concerning Religion, but even to such as were indifferent, which they communicated not without much trouble. For *Strabo* affirms, that the 13 Years, during which *Plato* and *Eudoxus* continued at *Heliopolis,* were not simply spent by them in learning Astronomie, but in courting the favour and friendship of the Priests, that they might be thereby induced to teach them something of what they knew in that Science. If they were so shie in communicating to others what they had observed in the Heavens, and which any others might have seen as well as they; it may well be imagined they much more carefully concealed the Historie of their Countrie: so that it is not to be admired there is so little come to our knowledge of what passed there before the Conquest made by the *Persians.* Nay, if the *Ethiopi-*

ons had commanded there before, and that for a long tract of time, as *Herodotus* mentions, it is likely that even then the Sources of the *Nile* were not unknown, nor the causes of its Inundation. And who knows whether in the time of *Herodotus* the Priests knew not more of those things then they would communicate to him? For if they had relations of a Voyage of 4 Monteths, that is, above 1200 Leagues, continually ascending, partly upon the *Nile,* partly on the sides of it beyond the Tropick of *Cancer,* those who had made it must have passed all the *Torrid Zone,* and found the source and origine of the *Nile.* But they said, that in those Countries the *Nile* flowed from West to East, and not from South to North, as it did in *Aegypt;* which is not consonant to the reason given by *Herodotus* himself of the overflux of that River; nor the Modern Geographies, according to which the Sources of the *Nile* are far beyond the *Equinoctial Line.*

This then passing for certain, with a length of the course of the *Nile* equal to that attributed thereto by *Herodotus,* methinks there might be a reason found out of its overflowing in *Aegypt* more probable then those which many have hitherto given thereof. For what makes the overflux miraculous is, that it happens, as we have already said during the great heats of Summer, when all other Rivers are at the lowest or dryed up: which occasioned a perswasion, that it proceeds from a cause different from that of others, which manifestly depend on the Rains which fall, and the Snow which ordinarily melts in great abundance towards the end of Winter, at which time the *Nile* is at the lowest. Some therefore have been of opinion, as *Herodotus* relates, that the *Nile* overflows in Summer, because then there come into *Aegypt* continually certain Winds called the *Etesian* from the Northern Coast, which obstruct its course, and so croud up its Waters, depriving them of the freedom of falling into the Sea, as they ordinarily do, as the reflux of the *Ocean* daily does the Rivers which fall into it. Others attributed the cause of it to the *Ocean,* out of which they affirmed the *Nile* to take its origine; but they explicated not after what manner this was done. Others affirmed, that this overflux proceeded from the Snow, which they pretended was dissolved in Summer upon the sides of the *Nile. Herodotus* refutes all these conjectures, and then gives his own opinion, which is, that the *Nile* coming from some very remote parts of the *South*, that is, from a Countrey from which the Sun is far distant in Summer, when it is very near *Aegypt* its course, which at its coming out of the source is always equally big, comes then quite to *Aegypt* without losing any thing of its fulnesse, in regard the Sun consumes nothing or very little of it: whereas in Winter it decreases much by the way, for the contrary reason; which is that the Sun being then directly upon its waters devours a great part thereof. *Strabo,* who thought not this reason of *Herodotus* more probable then the others, recurs to that which he says had been observed by *Homer,* when he called *Aegypt* (that is to say the *Nile* in *Homerical* terms) a River falling from Heaven.

He would therefore have the overflux of the *Nile* proceed from the Summer-rains, which (saith he) are frequent in *Ethiopia,* according to their Relation who have sailed on the Red Sea as far as the Countrey which produces *Cinnamon,* as also of those who have been at the Hunting of Elephants. The Relation of the Monk *Cosmas,* inserted by the most Learned and Ingeniously curious person Monsieur *Thevenot* in the First Part of his *Collections,* says methinks the same thing. But, besides that the sources of the *Nile* are at a far greater distance then is supposed by that reason alledged also by our Author in its proper place, there is no great likelihood that the rains should be so frequent in Summer in a Countrey next adjoyning to *Aegypt,* where it never rains, and more Southerly then it. Whence it comes that at this time the ablest Philosophers endeavours to find out some other cause of so considerable an effect, and Monsieur *de la Chambre* among others by an extraordinary sagacity hath found out one, for it in the Bowels of the Land of *Aegypt,* whose Nitrous qualities stirred by the heats of Summer are in his judgement capable of causing the Waters of that River to rise up to so great an overflux, as we see by experience that it does. This opinion, when we shall have comprehended the subtile Discourses, and considered the excellent remarks whereby that great great person confirms it, will doubtless be found the most likely to be true.

Monsieur *Chapelain,* to whom most of the *Virtuosi* do now give an account, not onely of their works, but also of their designs, out of the confidence they have of his excellent judgment and sincere advice, told me not long since, that the most Learned and most Eloquent Monsieur *Vossius* hath a Treatise ready on the same Subject, wherein we are like to meet with many things yet unknown to us.

To make it appear then that I have also made some reflections on this Miracle, I shall here set down the reason I have imagined to my self for it, which does not contradict *Homer,* though it agrees not with *Strabo;* for it will haply suffice those who may not have the leisure to examine such as are more subtile. I observe then in the first place, that to my thinking it is affirmed by *Macinus,* that the risings of the *Nile* are framed above *Aegypt.* For towards the end of his forty eighth *Chaliph,* he says that the *Nile* being very low in the time of *Michael* Patriarch of *Alexandria,* that Prelate was sent by the *Mustanser, Choliph* of *Aegypt,* to the King of the *Abyssines,* who upon his intreaty having cleared the passage of the Water, it rose in *Aegypt* three Cubits in one night, and came to its height. I suppose next the two propositions by me already alledged, That the sources of the *Nile* are far beyond the Equinoctial Line; and, That its course thence into *Aegypt* is in length above twelve hundred leagues, that is fourteen of fifteen hundred: I suppose further, that at the Sources of the *Nile,* as in many other places, the Waters are higher in Winter then in Summer, according to what is affirmed by *F. Maffaeus* in his first Book of the *History of the Indies,* where he has this passage; *Processit ad ostium ingentis Fluvii, qui exipsis* Nili *fontibus originem trahens, Zaires ab incolis dicitur; actanta aquarum vi, praesertim hyeme, sese in Oceanum infert, ut prodatur in octaginta millia passuum ab eo vinci mare.* I suppose moreover, that the Waters of the *Nile,* when they are high, advance within the Chanel wherein they flow at about the rate of four leagues a day, according to what observation I have made upon the like occasion. For those who have seen the *Nile* overflown in *Aegypt* have assur'd me, that its course is about the same rate of swiftnesse as that of the *Seine* when it is in the same condition at *Paris.* Now the waters of the *Seine,* and the Rivers falling into it, according to my computation, when they are risen, make about the same measure of way every day. For at *Montereul* in *Normandy,* where I writ this, we have a small River which is of that number, and into which there come Waters, when it is high, from about four leagues distance, though its ordinary current comes but from the Spring of *Ternant*, distant from it but a league and a half. When this little River rises of a sudden by a storm, as it happens often, and that sometimes even in Summer the Waters are up but one day at *Montereul;* which argues that those which come last are a day in running the four leagues whence they come. There passes by *Cernieres,* which is but half a league from the same place, another small River, into which there come Waters from a distance double to the other; whence it comes that they are up two days, whereas they are but one at *Montereul.* In the last Inundation of the *Seine,* which was great and sudden enough at the end of Winter in the Year 1665, by reason of the abundance of Snow which was dissolved in a short time, I observed, being then at *Paris,* that the Waters began to rise the 18th. day of *February,* and continued till the end of that Moneth; after which they notably decreased till the 10th. of *March;* which discovers that the last-arrived were twenty days coming from the places where the Snow was dissolved. Those places I conceive to be about fourscore leagues from *Paris,* and consequently those Waters had advanced about four leagues a day.

All this supposed, I say for example, that the Waters which cause the overflowing of the *Nile* this day being the first of *August* in *Aegypt,* were got together in the places where its course began about a Year before, whether occasioned by Rain or Snow melted. Wherein there is nothing Miraculous or extraordinary. For at that time it was Summer in *Aegypt,* as it is this day; and consequently at the same time it was Winter in those Places, where the current of the *Nile* begins; since the Sources of it are at a great distance beyond the Equinoctial Line, where the Seasons are directly contrary to those which are on this side it. The Waters therefore were then about those Sources higher then at any other Season: but having fourteen or fifteen hundred leagues to advance ere they got to *Aegypt,* after the rate of about four leagues a day, they were about a year by the way; and consequently there could not be an overflux of the *Nile* in that Province sooner then now. And if it be true that the *Ganges* overflows also in Summer, as

Pliny and Modern Relations seem to affirm, and that consequently it is now in the same condition in the *Indies* as the *Nile* is in *Aegypt,* the cause may haply be the same. For its course being but half the length of that of the *Nile,* there needs but six Moneths for the Waters to get from the Sources to their Mouths, it being supposed those of the *Nile* take up a whole Year. Now it was Winter six Moneths before at the Sources of the *Ganges,* which are on this side the Equinoctial Line; as it was a Year ago at the Sources of the *Nile,* which are beyond it. The same is to be said of the River *Menam.*

As to the long continuance of the overflux of the *Nile,* which is a hundred days according to *Herodotus,* or rather six Moneths according to the same Author in another passage, where he says that in his time the water flowed out of the *Nile* into the Lake *Myris* or *Moeris* during the space of six Moneths, and returned out of the same Lake into the *Nile* at the same place whereat it had entred into it, during the other six Moneths of the Year; this continuance (I say) hath no other cause according to this position, but that which prolongs the Inundations of other Rivers. For it proceeds partly from the length of time that the Snow is dissolving, or the Waters falling, and partly from the different distance of the place from which they come into the Chanel of the *Nile* after the dissolving or falling. For thence it comes, that some get a long time after others from the place of their Rendezvous, and consequently they come in like manner into *Aegypt.*

We see also in all other Rivers something like the overflowings of the *Nile.* For many times the *Seine* for example is high and overflows at *Paris,* when no rain has fallen thereabouts, nor any Snow dissolved; and it is ordinarily some days after the Rain is past, or the Snow dissolved, when the weather is fair and clear, that its overflux is in its greatest force and height.

Moreover, That the Waters which cause the augmentations of the *Nile,* and its Inundations in *Aegypt,* come from the Torrents, the slime which they bring along with them, seem to testifie it. For the Waters which come from running Springs by ordinary Chanels are not muddy. It may also methinks be inferred from the same slime, that those Torrents force their way through cultivated and manured Lands; for the Waters which fall from the Sky upon Desert and Untilled places are pure and clear in their descent thence. If this be true, with the conjectures we have mentioned before, it must follow that the Meridional parts of *Africk* were inhabited and cultivated before *Aegypt* was in the World; and that being granted, if the Nitre of *Aegypt* be of the nature of our Saltpeter, which is framed of old Manure amass'd, and fermented a long time together, it might seem to be rather an effect then a cause of the overflowing of the *Nile*.

But haply we have said too much of the *Nile* and *Aegypt* in a Preface, which was to serve only for an Introduction to what is said thereof by our Author, of whom the Reader might expect we should give some account, though we have nothing to say of him, but only what may be conjectured by the Reading of his Book; according to which he was (as I conceive) of *Cairo*, that is to say, of *Masre*; for thus is that Famous City called to this day by its Inhabitants, as we have already observed: and the name of *Cairo*, under which it is known in *Europe*, came to it from that which the *Mugazzoldinil*, after he had conquered *Aegypt*, caused to be built near it for the Quartering of his *Militia*; and, which he called *Cahire* or *Cahre*, that is to say, the *Victorious* or *Conqueress*, either for the reason given thereof by *Macinus* in the Year 362, or in regard that being the Habitation of the Soldiery, it subdued in effect, and caused its Commands to be obeyed, not only by the Neighbouring City, but also by the whole Empire of the *Phatimite Chaliphs*, as the Camp near *Rome* in the time of the *Roman* Emperors, Commanded both the City and the Empire, and many times the Emperour himself. Our Author then, as far as I can conjecture, was of the same Countrey with *Macinus*, and lived about the same time, that is above four hundred Years since. For methinks he speaks of the Sultan the *Macolcamel*, the Son of *Abubeker*, the Son of *Job*, as of a Prince Reigning in his time; and he mentions not any other that Reigned since, though he speaks of divers who had Reigned before.

The esteem which the *Arabians* have at this day for his work sufficiently appears in my judgment by the beauty of the Copy, out of which we have made this Translation, and which was communicated to us by the late Cardinal *Mazarine*'s Library keeper, by the favour of Monsieur *Colbert*, who amidst his infinite cares for what concerns the Glory of his Majesty, and the happiness of his Subjects, is some times pleased to think on our *Arabian* Muses, and forgets not our labours in the distribution of the Favours which he obtains from his Majesty, for those who seriously apply themselves to the noblest kind of Learning. The Manuscript of the *Onirocrit Mussulman*, whereof we have lately published the Translation, was put into our hands by Monsieur *de Montmor*, principal Master of Requests, a Person as Eminent for his great Wit and rare Learning, as his Quality. I am glad to make this Discovery, for their satisfaction who were desirous to know whence I had it, and that it might be an acknowledgement of the kindnesses I have received from that Person upon that and divers other occasions.

But to return to our *Aegypt*: Were there nothing but the History, or rather the Fable, of *Gebirus* and *Charoba*, and the Nymph *Marina*, which is about the middle of this Work, I should not repent me of the Translation of it; for I little imagined to find in a *Mussulman* Author any thing so much allyed to the witty Fables of the ancient *Greek* and *Latine* Poets, as that Narration is, which made me reflect at the Translation of it on the midst of the fourth Book of the *Odyssey*, and the end of the fourth Book of the *Georgicks*. I have made the Title to my Translation according to the proposal of the Author, for it is not in the *Arabian* Manuscript. Nor is the name of the Author in the first Page of it, but I meet it in some other places, as the Reader may observe.

The *Pyramids* several times mentioned in it are expressed in the *Arabian* Tongue by two Names, to wit *Birba*, which I have used in several places; and *Haram*. The word *Birba*, and in the plural *Barabi*, is haply a corruption of *Pyramis*. Whether it be so or not, our Author calls so either the *Pyramids* in general, or only the least of them exclusively from the greatest, to which he particularly gives the other name, which is *Haram*, and in the *Arabian* signifies an *Old Structure*. Monsieur *Thevenot* hath given us in the first part of his *Collections* a most exact Description of those great *Pyramids* made by an *English*-man, who hath seen them in our time, and considered them at leisure; according to which those Structures consist of a certain number of square Foundations or Platforms set one upon another, all equal in thicknesse, but the upper Platform perpetually somewhat less in length and breadth then that which is under it, and set just up on the midst of it; the differences of length and breadth being every where equal between them, as also the depth or thicknesse: so that the whole *Pyramid* is only a square blunt point, the four sides whereof are Stairs, and the upper extremity is the least in length and breadth of all the Platforms whereof it confists. Which argues in my judgement, that heretofore there were some *Colosses* or *Obelisks* placed on them, as it were on their Pedestals, according to what *Herodotus* expresly affirms of the two built in the midst of the Lake *Moeris*. The height of every *Pyramid* is equal to the side of its Basis, according to the same *Herodotus,* who assigns that of *Cheops* eight hundred foot in length, as many in breadth, and as many in height, so that it is as 'twere in the form of a Cube, and covers with its Basis near seven Acres of ground, according to our measure of *Normandy,* that is to say, above thirteen furlongs; being all built of Free-stone, the least piece whereof was thirteen foot.

As to the City of the *Black Eagle,* whereof our Author promises to speak, I know not which it is, if it be not that *Outiratis,* in the Description of which he makes mention of the Figure of a *Black Eagle* set up on one of its Gates. If the name of the City of *Gainosamses,* that is to say, the *Eye* or *Fountain of the Sun,* be not understood of the Fountain of *Ammon,* or of the Lake called the *Fountain of the Sun, Fons Solis,* it seems to express that of *Heliopolis,* whose situation is answerable to that of *Masre,* and not to that of *Memphis. Masre* was also called *Fustata* in the time of *Gamrou,* the Son of *Gasus,* for the reason given thereof by *Macinus* in the Year *Twenty*. The *Danae* seems to be the Labyrinth. *Alphiom* is one of those Islands in the Continent, which *Strabo* calls *Anases,* and which are cultivated places, but surrounded on all sides by great Deserts. There are many of these *Anases* in *Africk,* and three particularly in *Aegypt,* in one whereof was heretofore the Oracle of *Jupiter Ammon*.

THE *PRODIGIES* OF EGYPT
According to the *ARABIANS*.

I*n the Name of God, gracious and merciful, I have learn'd a good word (says the Author of this Book, to whom God be merciful) of our Master the Prelate, the Guardian,* Abutachar Achamed *the Son of* Mahumet, *the Son of* Achamed, *the Son of* Abrahim, *the Son of* Solpha *the* Solphian, *the* Ispahanian, *God grant him mercy; who affirm'd that he had it from the mouth of the Apostle of God himself, whose memory be blessed, by Tradition from many great persons whom he named, as having received it one from another*; "Every man who hath a design, and begins not the prosecution of it with the praise of God, is either dumb, or incapable of compassing his Enterprize."

Let us therefore praise the great, eternal, immortal, and most wise God, who hath created all things by hill omnipotence, to be an experiment and demonstration of his Supreme Authority, to express his Unity, and conduct them to the knowledge of himself. There is not any thing like him; he understands all things, he sees all things. I would acknowledge that there is no other God then that great God alone, who has no companion, in the same manner as they acknowledge who serve their Lord sincerely, not imagining any thing equal to him. I shall also acknowledge that Mahumet *is Servant and Apostle, sent by him at a time when the World wanted some to be sent, and such Masters as should teach it the Rules of Religion, according to the footsteps of the Apostles, to persuade Nations. God favour him with his benedictions as also those of his House, who are holy and pure, and generally all those of his Party.*

As to this Book, I have set down in it the Excellencies of the City of Alexandria, *its Prodigies and Advantages. I make mention in it of the City of the Black Eagle, the cause of its building, and whatever there is miraculoas in it. I declare in it the Excellencies of* Egypt, *and her* Coptites, *and her* Nile, *and the Aliments she produces, as well by Land as by Sea; and of her Fruits, and the use made of them in every moneth of the year; and of the Extent thereof. I pray God that he would graciously enable me to relate what miraculous things her Sages, and Kings, and her* Pharaoh's, *and her Magicians, and her Priests, have wrought; and what* Talismans, *and what rare and extraordinary things they have set up: to treat of their Habitations, how they lived in them; and of their Wealth, how they acquired it, and secured it in their Pyramids built over it, and how they died, and left it behind them. To the end that they who are desirous to be instructed by Examples, may meet with some in their tracks; and that such as teach others may find Advertisements to give them, since this is it which is recommended to us by God, when he speaks thus in his Book;* "Have they not sojourn'd upon earth, and seen the end of those who were before them, more powerful then they, who tilled the ground, and cultivated it more then they, and who have seen their Apostles come to them with evident signs?" *and in several other the like passages of the* Alcoran.

The Priests of *Egypt*

It is affirmed that the most learned Priests, who excell'd in the noblest knowledge of Divination, and were most illuminated in that Art, were the Priests and Sages of *Egypt*. The Wise men of *Greece* are of that opinion, and affirm on their behalf, that in their Divinations they were inclin'd to Astrology, that they invented the occult Sciences, and knew hidden Secrets, that they made famous *Talismans,* and noble Laws; that they were the Authors of speaking Works and moving Figures; that they raised high Structures, and grav'd their Sciences on the hardest stones, which were then soft, like Earth water'd, or Paste; that they particularly excell'd in the Structure of Pyramids exactly built, on which they made exquisite *Talismans,* by means whereof they kept their Enemies from entering into their Cities and Provinces, by that means giving a clear demonstration of the Prodigies of their Science, and discovering the effects of their Wisdom. *Egypt* was then (they say) divided into fourscore and five Provinces, whereof there were forty five in the lower part, and forty in the upper. And in every Province there was a Governour taken from among the Princes of the Priests, who are they of whom God speaks in the History of *Pharaoh*, when he says, "*Send Heralds through the cities, to bring unto thee all the learned Magicians*": he means those Governours. They say that the Cities of the Princes of the Magicians were built by *Busiris*. The Priest who served the Stars was seven years in that Imployment; and when he was come to that degree, they called him *Cater,* as much as to say, *Master of the Influences;* and then he sate in the same Seat with the King, and the King led his Beasts to the Watering-place, and brought them back; that is, *did all his business* according to his counsel. When he saw him coming, he rose up to receive him, went to meet him, and made him sit down. Then the Priests approched, and with them the Masters of the Arts, who stood beneath the *Cater*. Every Priest served one particular Star, and was not permitted to serve any other; and he was called the Servant of such a Star, as the *Arabians* served every one his own God, and were called *Gabdosamse, Gabdiagoth, Gabdolgasi;* that is, Servant of *Samse,* or the Sun, Servant of *Jagoth,* Servant of *Gasi.* The *Cater* said to the Priest, Where is now the Star which thou servest? The Priest replied, It is in such a Sign, such a Degree, such a Minute. Then he put the same question to another; and when all had answered, and that he knew the Position of all the Stars, he addressed himself to the King, and said thus to him; It is requisite that you do such a thing to day, that you send an Army to such a place, that you clothe your self after such a manner, that you speak at such a time; and so of all he thought fit to be done in all the Kings Affairs, and in all the Government of the Kingdom. The King writ down all the *Cater* said, and whatever he disapprov'd. Then he turn'd to the Artists, and said thus to them; Grave thou such a Figure on such a Stone; and, Plant thou such a Tree; and to another, Make thou a Geometrical Draught of such a Work: and so to all from the first to the last. Immediately they all went every one to his

The *Cater*.

Shop, and beset themselves to do the works enjoyned them, exactly following the design propos'd to them by the *Cater*. They set down that day in a Register the Works performed therein; and the Register was folded up, and kept in the Kings Treasury. Their Affairs were dispatch'd according to this order: then the King (when he had any Affair) assembled the Priests without the City *Memphis,* and the People met together in the Streets of the said City. Then they made their entrance one after another in order, the Drum beating before them to bring the people together; and every one made some miraculous discovery of his Magick and Wisdom. One had, to their thinking who look'd on him, his Face surrounded with a light like that of the Sun, so that none could look earnestly upon him. Another seem'd clad with a Robe beset with Precious stones of divers colours, green, red or yellow, or wrought with gold. Another came mounted on a Lion, compass'd with Serpents like Girdles. Another came in cover'd with a Canopy or Pavilion of light. Another appear'd surrounded with Fire, turning about him so as that no body durst come near him. Another was seen with dreadful Birds perching about his Head, and shaking their wings like black Eagles and Vultures. Another made appear before him in the air dreadful and terrible persons, and winged Serpents. In fine, every one did what was taught him by the Star he served; yet all was but Apparition and Illusion without any reality: insomuch that when they came up to the King they spake thus to him; *"You imagin'd that it was so or so, but the truth is that it was such or such a thing."*

The Magick of the *Egyptian* Priests.

***Gancam* King and Priest commands Spirits to build him a Palace.**

There was heretofore in ancient *Masre* (which is *Emsos*) a King-Priest named *Gancam,* of the race of *Gariac* the Son of *Aram,* of whom the ancient *Egyptians* tell several stories, part whereof are beyond all likelihood. He liv'd before the Deluge, which he by his Science foresaw; whereupon he commanded the *Dæmons* who accompanied him to build him a Palace beyond the Equinoctial Line, which the ruines of this Universe could not reach. They built the Castle seated on the descent of the mountain of the Moon, which is the Castle of Brass, where are the Brazen Statues, in number LXXXV; out of the Throats whereof issues the Water of the *Nile,* which falls into a Fen full of Gravel, whence the water of the *Nile* flows into *Egypt* and other Climats, distributed and proportionably compass'd; for were it not for that it would spread over the greatest part of the Earth. The Spirits having built him that Castle, he had the curiosity to see it, and make his abode therein. To that end he sate in a Pavilion made purposely with much artifice, and the Spirits carried him on their shoulders to the Castle; where having consider'd the excellency of the Structure, and beauty of its Walls, with the Sculptures and the Paintings that were about it, and the Figures of the Celestial Bodies, and divers other wonderful things; for in the greatest obscurity of the night people saw clearly without Torches. There were Tables set and spread with all sorts of Meat, yet none perceiv'd to set them there; so all sorts of Drinks in vessels of Marble, Gold, and Silver, which he made use of; yet were they not increased or diminished. In the middest of the Castle there was a Cistern of Water congeal'd into Ice, whereof the motion might be perceived through that part which was frozen; as one sees through a Glass what is contained in it. Having considered all this, he was astonished thereat, and immediately returned into *Egypt;* where he left for his Lieutenant and Successour his Son *Gariac,* recommending his Subjects to him, and the Government of the Kingdom; and then he return'd to the Castle, and continued there till he died. He is thought to be Author of the Books of the *Coptites,* out of which they take their stories, and all that is to happen till the end of the World.

The Priestess *Borsa*, and her *Acts*.

In these Books of the *Coptites* there is mention made among other Princes of the Priestess *Borsa,* who administered justice to the people sitting in a Throne of Fire; so that when any one came for justice, if his cause were just, and he spoke the truth, the Fire returned to her; if on the contrary he were a lyar and deceiver, and came near the Fire, he was presently burnt thereby.

This Princess appear'd to men in divers forms as she pleased her self. She afterwards caused a Castle to be built on the side of the *Roman* Sea, to which she retir'd, and kept out of the sight of men. In the Walls of this Castle she caused to be put Pipes of Brass, the ends whereof came out and were hollow, having each written on them a representation of the several differences which ordinarily happen between men, and upon which they were went to desire Justice of her. When therefore any one was at difference with another, he came along with his Adversary to the Pipe on which was written the species of their difference, and spoke to it concerning his business very low, alledging all he could, then putting his Ear thereto he receiv'd an answer, which would be fully to all he desired. This custom continued constantly among them, till *Nabuchodonozor* over-ran *Egypt*. This Princess caused also to be made a *Ram* of a hard red Stone, and to be placed on a Pedestal of the same. Then she caused to be put on the Pedestal an Iron Pivot, and the upper stone to be pierced, on which was placed the Figure of the *Ram,* so that the Pivot appeared above; and she caused to be set on the top of the Pivot a Brazen Boat, the fore part whereof was made like the head of a Cock, and the hinderpart like the tail of the same Bird. This Mill-stone as it were turned with the *Ram* by regular and just motions. She caused this to be set on the descent of the Mountain, on which was afterwards built the great *Mosquey* of the Son of *Toulon,* to whom God shew mercy whence it is still called the Mountain of the *Ram,* and it will ever be called so. When therefore any enemy came to assault *Egypt* this *Ram* turned as the Mill-stone, and stopp'd towards that side that the Enemy was coming, and at the same time that Cock crew. She also caused to be built in the midst of the City a House of Adamant, wherein she put the Figures of all the Kings of the Earth which surround *Egypt*. She caused the Gates of that House to be Fortified, and set Guards at them, which were relieved in their turns, yet did not any but they enter into it or come near it. When therefore the *Ram* stopped of any side, and that they were assured that the King of that Countrey was in the Field, they opened the Gate of that House, and went to look for the Figure of that King, which immediately fell a shaking;

whence they inferred that he had a design to attaque *Egypt*. Then those Guards took the Halberds they had with them, and Swords made by Magick, and kept in that House, and fell a pricking that Figure with those Halberds, and to cut it with those Swords, and thereupon the Army of that King which came to spoil the Land of *Egypt* fell into such disorder, that the Souldiers killed one another, so that not one remained, and the King was forced to return without doing any thing. For that reason did the Kings respect and fear the Land of *Egpyt,* for not any did attempt the attaquing of it, but he came off with loss and disorder. Thus they were governed till the King of the *Greeks, Nabuchodonozor,* ingaged in a War against *Egypt* for the Reasons which we shall mention hereafter, if Almighty God give us the grace to do it. Dissention arose among his Souldiery, so that they all destroy'd one another; and he was forc'd to return from *Egypt* without doing any thing. He afterwards continued many years using all manner of Artifices, and making great expences, till he put a stop to those motions; after which he returned into the Land of *Egypt,* destroy'd the Inhabitants of it, and so ruined it, that the marks of it will continue to the end of the world.

Gariac the Son of King *Gancam* made himself also a Priest after his Father, and

The Brazen Tree.

did many wonderful things: and among others he made a Brazen Tree, which had branches of Iron, with sharp Hooks at the ends of them; which Tree when any unjust or lying person approached, those Hooks immediately flew at him, and fastened on his body, and could not by any means be gotten thence, till such time as he said the truth of his own accord, confess'd his injustice, and ceas'd injuring his Adversary. He also made an Idol of an hard black stone, which he named *Gabdopharouis,* that is, *Servant of Saturn*. Men came to declare their differences to that Idol, and demand justice of it; whereupon he who was in the wrong was staid in the place where he was, and could not get thence till he had done justice of himself; which if he did not, he would die in the place. When any one had some business or affair of great importance, he went to the Idol, and burnt about it certain Perfumes which they knew, then he lifted up his eyes to the Stars and named King *Gariac,* intreating and crying out, and immediately the *Dæmons* did the business for him. Sometimes *Gariac* was carried in the air by great Birds, and pass'd before his Subjects, who saw him with their eyes. When he was incens'd against any Nation which gave him any trouble in his Kingdom, he secretly sent among them some people, who cast into the water they drank certain things, which made it as bitter as the water of the Salt Sea, so that they could not taste of it. Sometimes by his Magick he gave the Beasts of the earth power over them, as Lions and Reptiles, which tore them to pieces.

Philemon also was one of the most considerable Priests of *Egypt,* whose story we shall relate in its proper place with that of *Noah,* if Almighty God give us the grace to do it.

Among the Priests of *Egypt* there was also the Priest *Saiouph,* who was he to whom they kindled the dreadful Fire, which he came near and spoke over it; then there came forth a great and terrible Figure, which acquainted them with whatever was necessary for them. This Priest *Saiouph* liv'd till the time of King *Pharaan,* in whose Reign the Deluge happened. He made his aboad in the Maritime Pyramid, which Pyramid was a Temple of the Stars, where there was a Figure of the Sun, and one of the Moon, both which spoke. The foremost or Meridional Pyramid was the Sepulchre of the Bodies of the Kings, to which *Saurid* was translated. There were within it several other admirable things, Statues, and Books, and among others the Laughing Statue, which was made of a green Precious Stone. They had dispos'd all these things within that place for fear of the Inundation and spoil.

The Maritime Pyramid.

As to the Priests who were in *Egypt* after the Deluge, there were a great number of them. The first who then follow'd that Profession was the Son of *Philemon,* who was imbarqu'd in the Ship with his Father and Sister, whom *Noah* married to *Bansar* the Son of *Cham,* which happened thus: King *Pharaan* sent the Priest *Philemon* to the Prophet of God *Noah,* to dispute with him about the Worship of the Idols; but *Philemon* by the grace and conduct of God believed in *Noah,* and confirm'd his Mission.

He afterwards imbarqued with him in the Ship, he and his Children, and seven of his Disciples, and after that gave his Daughter in Marriage to *Bansar* the Son of *Cham,* the Son of *Noah.* After they were come out of the Ship *Philemon* carried *Bansar* his Son in Law into *Egypt,* where his Daughter had by the said *Bansar* her Husband a Son, whom he named *Masar,* who was since King of *Egypt,* and caused it to be call'd *Masre* from his own Name, always worshipping one onely God, according to the Religion of *Noah.* The name of Priest was not then a reproach among them; for the Priest was then look'd upon as a Judge, who does not oppose the Laws prescribed unto him.

Divers Kings of Egypt.

The first who made an absolute profession of Priesthood in *Egypt,* who brought Religion into esteem, and applyed himself to the Worship of the Stars, was *Bardesir* the Son of *Cophtarim,* the Son of *Masar,* the Son of *Bansar,* the Son of *Cham,* for he was King after his Father; and it is reported that he made the great Laws, build the Pyramids, and set up for Idols the Figures of the Stars. The *Coptites* affirm that the Stars spoke to him, and many Miracles are attrited to him. Among other things it is said, he kept himself out of the sight of Men for several years of his Reign, appearing only from time to time, that is to say once a year, when the Sun entred into *Aries.* Then People came in to him, and he spoke to them, but they saw him not; afterwards he absented himself from them till the like time again, and then he gave them Commands and Prohibitions, yet so as that they saw him not with their Eyes. After a long time thus passed, he ordered to be built a Tower of Silver Gilt, and to be embellished with several Ornanaments; then he began to sit on it in a most Magnificent and Magestical form, and to speak to them. After that he went and sate before them in the Clouds in a Humane form; then he absented himself from them, save only when he discovered to them his Figure in the Temple of the Sun when the Sun entred in *Aries,* and ordered them to take for their King *Garim* the Son of *Cophtarim,* acquainting them that he would not return any more to them; wherein they obeyed him.

As to the Priestess *Bedoura,* she was a strong Woman, and as they say the Sister of *Bardesir,* and that he gave her his Art of Priesthood and Divination, whereupon she made most of the *Talismans* in the Pyramids. She also made the speaking Idols in *Memphis.* The Priesthood continued in her Family and Posterity, who received it successively one of another, and enjoyed its advantages. The *Egyptians* affirm that in her time the wild Beasts and the Birds hindered them from drinking the Water of the *Nile,* so that most of them dyed of Thirst, and that she sent against these Animals an Angel, who made so great a cry amongst them, that the Earth shook, and the Mountains were cleft. It is said, that by her Magick she fled in the Air, and that the Angels smote her with their Wings.

As for *Savan* the *Asmounian,* who they say was the ancient *Hermes;* he it was that built the House of the Statues, by which the measures of the *Nile* are know, and built to the Sun a Temple in the Province named *Basta;* and also ordered the building of *Asmounia;* and in the like manner that of the City of *Basre* in *Egypt,* which was twelve miles in length, above which he caused a Castle to be made. He also built *Danae,* where he established the Schools and the Recreations. 'Tis also said that he built the Pyramids of *Behansa,* where the women were in favour of his Daughter, and that he there erected Pillars, on which he raised a Tower of fine Glass, which might be seen from the City of *Gainosamse.* He also built on the descent of the Eastern Mountain in *Egypt* a City which he named *Outiratis,* that is in the *Coptick* Language, *The King's Favourite,* and put into it abundance of miraculous things. Among others he ordered four Pyramids to be made on the four sides of each Gate, and caused to be set on the Eastern Gate a Tower in the form of a Turret or Steeple, on which there was the Figure of a *Black Eagle*; and on

The City of the Black Eagle.

the Western Gate another Tower like the former, with the Figure of a *Bull*; on the Maritime Gate the like Tower, with the Figure of a *Lyon*; and on the outer or Southern Gate another such Tower, with the Figure of a Dog. He sent into these Figures Spirits that spoke; so that when any Stranger came into that City, at what Gate soever he entred, the Figure upon it made a noise, and the Inhabitants knew thereby that a stranger was come into their City, and immediately they seiz'd on him whereever he were. He planted there also a Tree which shaded the whole City, and bore all sorts of Fruits. He also raised in the midst of the City a high Watch-tower, the heighth whereof was fourscore Cubits, according to the measure of that time; and on the top of it a little Turret, which every day assum'd a different colour till the seventh day, after which it re-assumed its first colour, wherewith it filled the whole City. About this Watch-tower he disposed a great quantity of Water, wherein there was bred abundance of Fish. All about the City he set Talismans, which diverted all inconveniencies from the Inhabitants; and he called it the City of the *Jovians,* that is, Enchanters. There was in it for him a great Tower for the exercise of the Sciences of Magick, wherein he caused Assemblies to be made. It was seated on a mountain opposite to the City. God smote the Inhabitants of it with the Pestilence, so that they all died, and so ruin'd it, that there is not any track of it to be seen.

As to the time when the Pyramids were first built in *Egypt,* Historians relate, that there was a King named *Saurid,* the Son of *Sahaloc,* three hundred years before the Deluge, who dreamt one night that he saw the Earth overturned with its Inhabitants, the Men cast down on their faces, the Stars falling out of the Heavens, and striking one against the other, and making horrid and dreadful cries as they fell. He thereupon awoke much troubled, and related not his Dream to any body, and was satisfied in himself that some great accident would happen in the World. A year after he dreamt again that he saw the Fixed Stars come down to the earth in the form of white Birds, which carried men away, and cast them between two great Mountains, which almost joyned together, and covered them; and then the bright shining Stars became dark and were eclips'd: he thereupon awaked extremely astonished, and entered into the Temple of the Sun, and beset himself to bathe his cheeks and to weep. Next morning he ordered all the Princes of the Priests and Magicians of all the Provinces of *Egypt* to meet

The Pyramids built by *Aclimon*

together, which they did, to the number of a hundred and thirty Priests and Southsayers, with whom he went aside and related to them his Dream, which they found very important and of very great consequence, and the interpetation they gave of it was that some great accident would happen in the World. Among others the Priest *Aclimon* who was the greatest of all, and resided always in the Kings Court, said thus to him:

"Sir, your Dream is admirable, and I my self saw another about a Year since, which frightned me very much, and which I have not revealed to any one." "Tell me what it was," said the King. "I dreamt, said the Priest, that I was with your Majesty on the top of the Mountain of Fire, which is in the midst of *Emsos,* and that I saw the Heaven sunk down below its ordinary Situation, so that it was near the Crowns of our Heads, covering and surrounding us, like a great Basin turn'd upside down; that the Stars were intermingled amongst Men in diverse Figures, that the people implored your Majesties succour, and ran to you in multitudes as to their refuge; that you lifted up your hands above your head, and endeavoured to thrust back the Heaven, and to keep it from coming down so low; and that I seeing what your Majesty did, did also the same. While we were in that posture extreamly affrighted, methought we saw a certain part of Heaven opening, and a bright light coming out of it; that afterwards the Sun rose over us out of the same place, and we began to implore his assistance, whereupon he said thus to us, 'The Heaven will return to its ordinary situation, when I shall have performed three hundred courses.' I thereupon awaked extreamly affrighted."

The Priest having thus spoken, the King commanded them to take the heights of the Stars, and to consider what accident they portended. Whereupon they declared that they promised first the Deluge, and after that Fire. Then he commanded that Pyramids should be built, that they might remove and secure in them what was of most esteem in their Treasuries, with the bodies of their Kings and their Wealth, and the Aromatick Roots which served them; and that they should write their wisdom upon them, that the violence of the Water might not destroy it: wherein they presently set themselves at work. The *Egyptians* relate in their Annals, that *Saurid* is he who himself caused the Pyramids to be built; and that inasmuch as after the death of his Father he follow'd his steps, causing the Provinces to be inhabited and cultivated, and Governing them well, administring Justice to the People, even to his own prejudice and that of his Domesticks, causing Temples to be built, and Statues, and Talismans to be erected, so that the People had a great love for him. In the *Upper-Egypt* he built three Cities, and did so many wonders therein, that it is not possible to relate them. He first regulated the Tribute in *Egypt,* and enjoined works on Artists according to their power. He also was the first who ordered Pensions out of his Treasuries for maimed and sick people. He caused to be made a *Mirrour* of all sorts of Minerals, wherein they saw all the Climats, where there was abundance of Provisions or Sterility, and what new accident happen'd in any of the Coasts of *Egypt.* This Mirrour was upon a high Turret of Brass in the midst of ancient *Masre,* which is *Emsos.* He also first ordered Registers to be made, wherein was set down every day's receipts and expences, and the augmentation or diminution thereof, and kept them in the Royal Treasuries; then when a Moneth was pass'd he caused all to be reduced into one total sum, which he also had kept in the Royal Treasuries, sealed with the Royal Seal; causing moreover to be graved on Stone what was to be graved thereon. He made very liberal gratifications to the Masters of Arts, and those who deserved something should be given them. He also set up in the midst of the City the Figure of a Woman sitting, made of green stone, with a little Child in her lap sucking. All women who were troubled with any disease came to that Idol, and set their hands on the breasts of it, and presently they were cur'd of their indisposition. When a Woman was in very hard labour, as soon as she set her hand on the little Childs head, she was immediately brought to bed with ease. If an unchaste Woman set her hand on the same Childs head, all her members shook so that she was not able to speak. He made also several other works, which were destroyed by the Deluge. Yet the *Coptites* affirm, that they were found again after the Deluge, and used and adored as Idols,

Saurid's **Mirrour.**

that their Figures are represented in all the Pyramids of *Egypt*, and their diverse names; that those who taught them were Disciples of the Priest *Aclimon*, who also shewed them all the other works in *Egypt*. We shall speak of them in their proper place with the assistance of Almighty God. *Saurid* did also other prodigious things in his time, and among others he made an Idol named *Becres*, consisting of a mixture of divers Medicinal drugs, which had a marvellous vertue in securing Mens bodies from all sorts of diseases and inconveniences. By means hereof they knew who should escape and who should die of their sickness, by certain signs which appeared in the Idol; so that they gave over using remedies to some, and endeavoured the curing of others. They washed the members of that Idol, and gave the washings thereof to the sick to drink, who were thereupon immediately eased of their pain. 'Twas he also built the two great Pyramids so famous in all Nations. For a great part of the Sages affirm they were built by *Sedad* the Son of *Gad*, and that he was interred in one of the two; but the Ancients of the *Coptites* and their Sages deny the *Gadites* ever entred into the Land of *Egypt*. They deny also the same thing of the *Amalekites*, and say that *Egypt* was always inaccessible to them, by reason of its Enchanters and their Artifices and Stratagems. The Learned relate in the Lives and Histories, that the Pyramids were built three hundred years before the Deluge. So speaks of them *Armelius*, Author of the Book of *Illustrious Men*. *Abumasar* the Astrologer, in his Book of *Thousands*, says that the reason of building the Pyramids was the Dream which *Saurid* the Son of *Sahaloc* saw. He confirms it in his Book of *Miraculous Dreams*, where he adds that he sent for the Priests and Southsayers of his time, and the Astrologers, and related to them what he had seen of the descent of the Moon upon Earth in the form of a Woman; of the overturning of the Earth with its Inhabitants, and of the total Eclipse of the Sun; and the dream he had after that: and that the Priests declared to him the coming of the Deluge, whereof mention is made in the Book of the *Annals*, which the *Egyptians* attribute to two Brothers *Coptites*, saying that

Pyramids built before the Deluge.

The Brothers Annals.

those two Brothers interpreted an ancient Book, which had been found in some one of their Sepulchres on the breast of a man. They say these two Brothers were the Children of a certain man of the Race of the ancient *Egyptians*, to wit, those who escaped the Deluge, and were embarqued with the Prophet of God *Noah*. We shall with the help of God say somewhat hereafter of the History of these two Brothers. It was found therefore in the Book they Translated, that *Saurid* the Son of *Sahaloc*, King of *Egypt*, after he had seen his dreams and related them to the Priests, and that *Aclimon* had also related his to him, commanded the Priests to see what remarkable events the influences of the Stars portended to the World; and that the Priests having exactly erected a Celestial Figure for the hour of his question, found that it signified a great mischief which was to descend from Heaven, and issue out of the Earth, which they declared unto him; whereupon he caused Pyramids and great Structures to be built, to serve for refuges to him and his Domesticks, and Sepulchres for the conservation of their Bodies; as also that they might engrave and mark on their Roofs, their Walls, and their Pillars, all the obscure and difficult Sciences, whereof the *Egyptians* made profession, learning them and treasuring them up as Illustrious Inheritances from those who were grown famous in all Nations: and that they should also represent on them the Figures of the Stars in their Signs, with their effects and significations, and the secrets of Nature, and the productions of Arts, and the great Laws, and the beneficial Drugs, and the Talismans, and Medicine, and Geometry, and all the other things that might be advantageous to men, as well for the publick as for private persons, clearly and intelligibly to those who were acquainted with their Books, their Language, and their Writings. King *Saurid* knew certainly that the calamity was to be general to all Countries in the World, or come very near it. Then he said to them, "When shall this great evil happen wherewith we are threatned?" Whereto they replyed thus: "When the heart of the *Lion* shall come to the first Minute of *Cancer*'s head, and the Planets shall be in their Houses, in those places of the Sphere, the Sun and Moon in the first minute of *Aries; Pharouis,* who is *Saturn,* in the first degree; *Raouis,* which is *Jupiter* in *Pisces* at 27 degrees 3 minutes; *Mars* in *Libra,* and *Venus* in *Leo* at 5 degrees and some minutes." Then he said to them, "See whether after this great evil there will happen any other accident in *Egypt."*

They consider'd and saw that the Stars portended another great misfortune, which was to descend from Heaven, contrary to the former, that is, a Fire that should consume the Universe. Whereupon he said to them; "When is that to happen?" They reply'd, "We have made our Observation, and found that it is to happen, when the heart of the *Lion* shall be at the end of the fifteenth degree of *Leo,* and that the Sun shall be with him in one minute joyning that of *Saturn; Jupiter* is direct in the *Lion,* and with him *Mars,* changing the minute; and the Moon in *Aquarius* near the *Dragons* Tail, at twelve parts. There will be at that time an Eclipse of the greatest congruence, *Venus* shall be at the greatest distance from the Sun, and *Mercury* the like." Then *Saurid* said unto them, "Is there yet any other great accident that you can fore-see besides those two remarkable evils?"

They look'd and found that when the heart of the *Lion* shall have compleated two thirds of his circle, there would not remain any Animal moving on the Earth, which should not be destroy'd; and that when he should compleat his revolution, the knots of the Sphere would be dissolved. The King was very much astonished at that, and commanded the great Pillars to be cut down, and that the great Pavement should be melted: he caused Tin to be brought out of the Western parts, then he made them take black stones, which he caused to be laid for the foundations of the Pyramids about *Syene.* They were brought from the *Nile* upon Engines, and they had certain particular impressions and marks, and upon them painted Billets, which the Sages had set there: so that when they had smitten the stone, it advanc'd of it self the space of a Flight-shot. These stones were set in the foundations of the Pyramids, to wit, of the first, which is the Eastern, and of the Western, and of the Coloured. They put in the midst of every piece an Iron Bar like a Pivot standing up, then they set on that another piece after they

The three Pyramids.

had made a hole through the middle of it, that the Iron Pivot might enter into it, and fasten it to that which was under; after which they melted Lead, and it was poured all about the piece, after they had adjusted the Writing which was above. He caused Gates to be made under ground, at four Cubits depth, according to their measure; which Gates had Sallies into vaulted Casemates built of stone, and fortify'd with much Artifice, and whereof the Situation was conceal'd, every Vault being fifty Cubits in length. The Gate of the Eastern Pyramid was on the South-side a hundred Cubits distant from the midst of the Western wall on the Western side. They measur d also from the Western wall, that is, from the midst of it a hundred Cubits, and they digg'd till they got down to the door of the vaulted Casemate, through which they entred into it. As to the Colour'd Pyramid, made of stones of two colours, the Gate of it was on the Maritime or North-side, and they measur'd also from the midst of the Maritime wall a hundred Cubits, which made five hundred, according to the *Mussulman* measure. He built it perpendicularly into the ground, to the depth of forty Cubits, then he raised it as much, though what is above ground of the Pyramids do not exceed the third part, so that this last is the highest, built after the manner of the raised Floors and high Rooms of our present time. They built them in the time of their good fortune, while all their Worldly concerns came according to their wishes. King *Saurid* having compleated the Structure, cover'd them with Silks of several colours from the top to the bottom, and caused a great Feast to be celebrated for them, whereto all the Inhabitants of the Kingdom came, not so much as one being wanting from all the Coasts of *Egypt*. Then he commanded them to make thirty *Gernes* or great Vessels of colour'd stone, which they excellently cast. He also ordered covers to be made of the same. Every Vessel held a hundred Mules load. He caused them to be set in the lowest Story of the Eastern Pyramid, and had brought thither precious Stones and Jacinths, till the Floor was full thereof. He caused the Vessels to be cover'd with their Covers, and Lead to be melted thereon; then he caused pieces of Gold and Silver to be scatter'd, as much as might divert their sight who should look on them. Then he caused to be brought thither all he could of his Treasures, and the most precious of his Wealth, Jewels, Plate, Precious Stones, cast and coloured Pearls, Vessels of Emerald, Vessels of Gold and Silver, Statues excellently wrought, Artificial Waters, Talismans, precious Iron that would twine about like Cloath, Philosophical Laws, the Nurses of Wisdom, divers sorts of Medicinal Drugs, exquisite Tables of Brass, on which divers Sciences were written; as also Poisons and Mortal drinks, which Kings have ready by them, and wholesome Preservatives and Antidotes; and several other things, which it is impossible to describe. But all this could not secure them from the evils wherewith God afflicted them for their Infidelity. In the mean time they imagin'd that their Fortresses would defend them against God; but God came to them on the side they were not aware of, and destroyed their great Flocks by the Deluge and other misfortunes: Praise be to him, he is the only and the Almighty God. All is perishable save onely his Majesty; to him belongs Wisdom, and to him you will return. After that, says the Author, King *Saurid* caused to be brought into the second Pyramid the Idols of the Stars, and the Tabernacles of the Celestial Bodies, and what Statues and Perfumes his Ancestors had caused to be made, by means whereof men had access to him, and their Books, and what Annals and Histories they had caused to be made for themselves of what had pass'd in their time, and of the predictions of what was to happen after them, to the Kings who should govern *Egypt* to the last times, and the state of the fixed Stars, and what was to happen by their repose and motions from time to time. Then he caused to be put into the third Pyramid the Bodies of the Kings and Priests in *Gernes,* or great Vessels of hard black Stone; and by every Priest his Book, and the Miracles of his Art and Life. He also caused to be set along the walls of the Pyramids Idols, which held in their hands all the Arts according to their ranks and measures, the description of each Art, and the manner of exercising it, and what was necessary for that, and in like manner the *Caters:* For the Priests were distinguish'd into seven Orders; the first whereof was that of the *Caters,* who were they that served all the seven Planets, every Planet seven Years. With the *Cater* was the Universal Doctor. The second Order was theirs who serv'd six Planets, and immediately followed after the first degree. After that they named that which served five of them, and under, the following and inferiour. Then he caused also to be brought into the third Pyramid the Bodies of the Masters of the Laws, with those of the Priests, and the wealth of the Houses of the Stars and their Ornaments, which they had had by Offerings, and the goods of the Priests. After that he appointed one of them for a Guard to each Pyramid. The Guard therefore of the Eastern Pyramid was an Idol of *Jamanick* shell, black and white, which had both eyes open, and sate on a Throne, having near it as it were a Halberd, on which if any one cast his eye, he heard on that side a dreadful noise, which made his heart faint, and he who heard that noise dyed. There was a Spirit appointed to serve that Guard, which Spirit never went from before it. The Guard of the Western Pyramid was an Idol of hard Red stone, having in like manner in his hand somewhat like a Halberd, and on his head a wreathed Serpent, which flew at those who came near him, clung about their necks and kill'd them. There was appointed to serve him an ugly deformed Spirit, which parted not from him. For Guard to the third Pyramid he had plac'd a small Idol of *Baby* stone, on a Basis of the same; which Idol drew to it those who look'd on it, and stuck to them till it had destroy'd them, or made them distracted. There was also a Spirit appointed to serve it, which parted not from it. *Saurid* having finish'd the building of the Pyramids, and compassed them with the bodies of Spiritual substances, he offer'd Sacrifices to them, and presented them with the Offerings chosen for them. The Spirits appointed for the service of each Star knew the Ascendant of the Stars they served, and they serv'd them according to their rank one after another. He distributed and appointed the names under which should be divided the Works that should be presented to them. The *Coptites* affirm, that King *Saurid*'s Name was written upon the first Pyramid, with the time spent in the building of it. Some say he had it built in six monaths, and that he defied those that came after him to demolish it in 600 years; though it be certain it is more easie to pull down

The Guards of the Pyramids.

then to build. He said also speaking to them themselves, "I have cover'd them with Silk, do you cover them if you can with Linen cloth."

But those who have reigned after him at several times, have seen that they were nothing in comparison of him, and that they could not cover them so much as with Mat, and with much ado should they have cover'd them with any thing else.

Stories of the Pyramids. As to the miraculous stories related of the *Pyramids,* the Author of that Book (God shew him mercy) says, that in the Annals contained in the Books of the *Egyptians,* and their Miracles, there is such plenty of admirable Histories, that it is impossible to relate them all: I shall onely (adds he) relate some of them, and among others this; The Commander of the Faithful, the *Mamunus,* God shew him mercy, being come into the Land of *Egypt,* and having seen he Pyramids, had a desire to demolish them, or at least some one of them, to se what was within it. Whereupon it was thus said to him; "You desire a thing which it is not possible for you to have. If you attempt it and fail, it will be a dishonour to the Commander of the Faithful."

Whereto he replied, "I cannot for bear but I must discover something."

He therefore put them to work at the breach, which was already begun, and made great expences therein. For they kindled fire on the stone, then they cast Vinegar on it, and afterwards batter'd the place with Engines. The breadth of the wall was 20 Cubits, according to the Geometrical measure. Being come to the upper story of the Pyramid, they found behind the breach a green Basin, wherein there were pieces of Gold weighing each of them an ounce, according to our ordinary Weights; and of those pieces there was just 1000. The Demolishers wonder'd at it, and brought the Gold to the *Mamunus,* not knowing what it meant. The *Mamunus* was also astonished at it, admiring the excellent Workmanship and good Alloy of the Gold. Then he said to them, Compute what expence you have made in the breach. They computed, and found that the expence equall'd the value of the Gold which they had found, so as that there was not a Farthing more or less. The *Mamunus* was yet more astonish'd at that, and said to those who kept his Accompts; "Consider the foresight of this Nation, and the greatness of their Science. Their Sages had told them that there would arise some one that should in some place open one of these Pyramids: they examined that, and computed what expence he should make who attempted that work, and set the summe at the place; that he who got thither, finding his account, and seeing he had not gain'd any thing, should not begin any such work again."

They say the Basin was made of a green Emerald, and that the *Mamunus* had it carried to *Gueraca,* where it was one of the noblest pieces of his Treasury.

Another History relates, that after the Pyramid was open'd people went in out of curiosity for some years, many entering into it, and some returning thence without any inconvenience, others perishing in it. One day it happened that a company of Young men (above 20 in number) swore that they would go into it, provided nothing hindered them, and to force their way to the end of it. They therefore took along with them meat and drink for two moneths: they also took Plates of Iron and Bars, Wax-candles and Lanterns, Match and Oyl, Hatchets, Hooks, and other sharp Instruments, and enter'd into the Pyramid: most of them got down from the first Descent and the second, and pass'd along the ground of the Pyramid, where they saw Bats as big as black Eagles, which began to beat their Faces with much violence. But they generously endur'd that inconvenience, and advanc'd still till they came to a Narrow passage, through which came an impetuous wind, and extra ordinary cold; yet so as they could not perceive whence it came, nor whither it went. They advanc'd to get into the Narrow place, and then their Candles began to go out, which obliged them to put them into their Lanterns. Then they entered, but the place seemed to be joyn'd and close before them: whereupon one of them said to the rest, "Tie me by the wast with a cord, and I will venture to advance, conditionally that if any accident happen to me, you immediately draw me back."

At the entrance of the Narrow place there were great empty vessels made like Coffins, with their lids by them; whence they inferr'd, that those who set them there had prepar'd them for their death; and that to get to their Treasures and Wealth there was a necessity of passing through that Narrow place. They bound their Companion with cords, that he might venture to get through that passage; but immediately the passage clos'd upon him, and they heard the noise of the crushing of his bones: they drew the cords to them, but they could not get him back. Then there came to them a dreadful voice out of that Cave, which startled and blinded them so that they fell down, having neither motion nor sense. They came to themselves awhile after, and endeavoured to get out, being much at a loss what to do. At last after much trouble they returned, save onely some of them who fell under the Descent. Being come out into the Plain they sate down together, all astonished at what they had seen, and reflecting on what had happened to them; whereupon the Earth cleft before them, and cast up their dead Companion, who was at first immovable, but two hours after began to move, and spoke to them in a Language they understood not, for it was not the *Arabian*. But some time after one of the Inhabitants of the Upper *Egypt* interpreted it to them, and told them his meaning was this; "*This is the reward of those who endeavour to seise what belongs to another.*" After these words their Companion seemed dead as before, whereupon they buried him in that place. Some of them died also in the Pyramid. Since that, he who commanded in those parts, having heard of their adventure, they were brought to him, and they related all this to him, which he much wondered at.

Another History relates, that some entered into the Pyramid, and came to the lowest part of it, where they turned round about. There appeared to them a Hollow place, wherein there was a beaten path, in which they began to go. And then they found a Basin, out of which distill'd fresh water, which fell into several Pits which were under the Basin, so as they knew not whence it came, nor whether it went. After that they found a square Hall, the walls whereof were of strange stones of several colours. One of the company took a little stone and put into his mouth, and immediately his ears were deafened. Afterwards they came to a place made like a Cistern full of coined Gold, like a large sort of Cakes that are made; for every piece was of the weight of 1000 Drams. They took some of them, but could not get out of the place till they had returned them into the place whence they had taken them. They afterwards found another place with a great Bench, such as is ordinarily before houses for people to sit on; and on the Bench a Figure of green stone, representing a tall ancient Man sitting, having a large Garment about him, and little Statues before him, as if they were Children whom he taught: they took some of those Figures, but could not get out of the place till they had left them behind them. They passed on along the same way, and heard a dreadful noise and great hurly-burly, which they durst not approach. Then having advanced further, they found a square place, as if it were for some great Assembly, where there were many Statues, and among others the Figure of a Cock made of red Gold: that Figure was dreadful, enamelled with Jacinths, whereof there were two great ones in both eyes, which shined like two great Torches: they went near it, and immediately it crew terribly, and began to beat its two wings, and thereupon they heard several voices which came to them on all sides. They kept on their way, and found afterwards an Idol of white stone, with the Figure of a Woman standing on her head, and two Lions of whte stone lying on each side of her, which seem'd to roar and endeavour to bite. They recommended themselves to God and went on, and kept on their way till they saw a Light; after which going out at an open place, they perceiv'd they were in a great Sandy Desert. At the passage out of that open place there were two Statues of black stone, having Half Pikes in their hands. They were extremely astonish'd, whereupon they began to return towards the East, till they came near the Pyramids on the out side. This happen'd in the time of *Jezid,* the Son of *Gabdolmelic,* the Son of *Gabdol,* Governour of *Egypt,* who having heard of it sent some persons with those before spoken of to observe the open place of the Pyramid. They sought it several days, but could never find it again, whereupon they were accounted fools. But they shew'd him the head of a Ring which one of them had taken in the

Assembly-place, which they had found in the Pyramid; which obliged him to believe what they said. That head was valued at a great summe of money.

It is further related, that other persons in the time of the Commander *Achemed,* the Son of *Toulon* (God shew him mercy) entered in like manner into the Pyramid, and found there a Cruse of red Glass, which they brought away. As they came out they lost one of their Men, which oblig'd them to go in again to look for him. They found him stark naked laughing continually, and saying to them, "Trouble not your selves to look for me." After which he got away from them, and return'd into the Pyramid. Whence they inferr'd that the Spirits had distracted him, whereupon they went out and left him there. Upon which they were accused before the Judge, who condemn'd them to exemplary punishment, and took away from them the Cruse, which had in it four pound of glass. A certain person said thereupon, that that Cruse had not been set in that place for nothing. Which occasioned the filling of it with water, and then being weighed again, it weighed as much as when it was empty, and no more. They afterwards took off some of that water several times, but the Vessel came still to the same weight. Whence they conjectured that it was one of the Wine-vessels whereof the Ancients had made use, and had been made to that purpose by their Sages, and placed there. For the use of Wine was permitted among them. This was a strange Miracle.

They relate further several Stories of this kind, and among others that some entered into the Pyramid with a Child to abuse it; and that having committed that sin, there came out against them a black young Man, with a Cudgel in his hand, who beat them furiously, so that they fled leaving there their Meat and their Cloaths. The same thing happen'd to others in the Pyramid of *Achemima.* There entered also into the Pyramid of *Achemima* a Man and a Woman to commit Adultery therein; but they were immediately cast along on the ground, and dyed in a Phrensie.

Predictions made to King *Saurid.*

When the Priests (says the Author) had told King *Saurid* of the great conflagration, which was to happen by Fire, and that that Fire should come out of the Sign *Leo;* he caused to be made in the Pyramids certain windings, which abutted upon narrow Vaults, which drew the Winds into the Pyramids with a dreadful noise. He also caused Chanels to be made therein, by which the Water of the *Nile* came in at the same place, then it retreated of it self, and return'd into the *Nile* by another passage, after the manner of the Cisterns which are made for the reception of Rain-water. He also caused certain Chanels to be made therein, which reach'd to certain places of the Land of the West, and to certain places of the Land of *Upper Egypt.* He fill'd those Subterraneous places with prodigious things, Statues, speaking Idols, and Talismans. Some *Coptites* affirm, that after the coming of the Deluge, and the Conflagration had been predicted to him, he said to the Astrologers; "Shall our Countrey suffer some part of these misfortunes?" "It shall (reply'd they) be afflicted with a desolation which shall continue so many years, that the Dragons and Vipers shall be so exceedingly multiplied therein, that none shall dare to pass through it." "And whence shall this desolation come?" said *Saurid.* "From the King of a remote Countrey, said they, who shall destroy its Inhabitants, and so ruine it, that the marks thereof shall remain eternally, clearly carrying away all its Wealth. But after that it shall be repeopled by his Son, born of one of his Bondwomen."

This King was *Nahuchodonozor,* who destroy'd *Egypt,* and whose Son *Balsas* (born of a Captive *Coptess)* repeopled it, and built there the Castle and the Church *Mugalleca,* or *Suspended.*

Nebuchodonozor.

"What shall happen after that?" said *Saurid* to the Priests. "There will come into *Egypt,*" replyed they, "a Nation of ugly and deformed People, from the Coast of the *Nile,* that is, from the Countrey whence it comes, which Nation shall possesse it self of the greatest part thereof." "After that," said he again, "what shall happen?" "Its *Nile* shall fail it," reply'd they, "and its Inhabitants shall forsake it. Then it shall be possessed first by a Barbarous Nation, whose language shall be unknown, and which shall come from the Eastern Coast; afterwards by another coming from the Western Coast, which shall be the last."

He commanded all this to be writ down, and that it should be graved on the Pyramids and Obelisks. One of the things which confirm this discourse by their consonancy is, that *Abucabil,* the *Mogapherian,* the Pacifier, related this to *Achamed,* the Son of *Toulon,* (God shew him mercy) when he entered into *Egypt.* With the help of God we shall speak of him hereafter.

The Spirits of the Pyramids.

As to the Spirits which are met in the Pyramids, and the like Structures, and the forms under which they appear, the Author (to whom God shew mercy) speaks of them briefly thus in a Chapter he hath expresly made of them: They relate, saith he, several things of the Pyramids, which would be long to declare; but as to the Spirits which reign over them, and such other Structures, named *Birba*'s, they say that the Spirit of the Meridional Pyramid never appears out of it, but in the form of a naked Woman, who has not even her privy parts covered, beautiful as to all other parts, and whereof the behaviour is such, as when she would provoke any one to love and make him distracted, she laughs on him, and presently he approches her, and she draws him to her, and besots him with love, so that he immediately grows mad, and wanders like a Vagabond up and down the Countrey. Divers persons have seen her walking about the Pyramid about Noon, and about Sun-set. One day she distracted one of the People of the *Chacambermille,* who was afterwards seen running stark naked through the streets without fear or wit. The Spirit of the second Pyramid, which is the Colour'd, is an ancient *Nubian,* having a Basket on his head, and in his hands a Censer like those used in Churches, wherewith he incenses about it at all the Obelisks. As to the *Birba* of *Achemima,* its Spirit is a Young Man, Beardless and Naked, sufficiently known among the Inhabitants of the place. The Spirit of the *Birba* of *Semir* is a black swarthy Old Man, of high Stature, and having a short Beard. The Spirit of the *Birba* of of *Phacat* appears in the form of a black young Woman, having in her arm a little black Infant deformed, shewing his Dogs teeth, and having his eyes all white. The Spirit of the *Birba* of *Ridousa* appears in the form of a Man, having the head of a *Lion* with two long Horns. The Spirit of the *Birba* of *Busira* appears in the form of an old white Monk carrying a Book. The Spirit of the *Birba* of *Gaphi* appears in the form of a Shepherd, clad in a black Robe, with a Staff in his hand. As to the Pyramids of *Dehasoura,* their Spirits are seen in the form of two black old Men. The Spirit of the *Birba* of *Samnos* appears in the form of a Monk, who comes out of the Sea, and views himself in it as in a Lookingglass. All these Spirits are manifestly seen by such as come near them, and the places of their retirement, and frequent there abouts along time. There are for all of them certain particular Offerings, by means whereof it is possible the Treasures of the *Birbas* and the Pyramids may appear, and that there may be a friendship and familiarity between Men and Spirits, according to what the Sages have establish'd.

Saurid the Son of *Sahaloc,* says the Author, continued King of *Egypt* a hundred and seven years. His Astrologers told him the time he should die, whereupon he made his last Will to his Son *Hargib,* told him whatever was necessary for him, and ordered him to have him carried into the Pyramid, and to have him disposed into the Tomb which he himself had caused to be made, that he should cover the bottom of it with Camphire and Santal-wood, and that he should enbalm his body with the drugs which prevent corruption, and that he should leave by him the richest of his Armour, and the most precious of his Housholdstuff. His Son performed all this after his death, and then *Hargib* Reigned after his Father in the Land of *Egypt,* and follow'd his footsteps, being careful as he had been to administer Justice to the People, to have the Countrey cultivated and inhabited, and to procure the wellfare of his Subjects, which obliged them to have a great affection for him. He afterwards caused to be built the first of the Pyramids of *Dehasoura,* and to be brought thither abundance of Wealth, and precious Stones of great value. *Hargib* was particularly addicted to Chemistry, to get Metals out of the Mines, and to gather money; he afterwards enterred every year a great quantity thereof, and minded not the putting of Statue and speaking Idols into his Pyramid. He a long time continued that exercise, during which he had a Daughter, who being grown up suffer'd herself to be debauched by one of his people, which obliged him to sent her away into the West, where he had a City built for her in the Countrey of *Barca.* This City being built they gave it the name of that Princess, which was as they say, *Domeria.* For he caused a Pilory to be built in the midst of the City, and her name to be grav'd on it: then he sent to live there with her all the old Women of his House. He continued King ninety nine years, then dyed: and was interred in the Pyramids. His Son *Menaos* Reigned after him in *Egypt,* and was a proud and hauty Prince, who spilt much blood, ill treated his Subjects, Ravished many Women, and squandered away a great part of the Treasures of his Ancestors. For he built Palaces of Gold and Silver, into which he brought Chanels of the *Nile,* the bottom whereof he caused to be covered with Jacinths and other precious stones instead of Sand. He tormented Men, and took away their goods and Cattel by force. This got him the hatred of the People, and at last the Beast he rid on threw him and broke his neck; (Gods curse go with him.) So God delivered the *Egyptians* of him.

History of the Deluge.

As to the History of the *Deluge,* and the adventures of *Noah,* to whom God grant peace and mercy, take in few words what is said thereof. They relate that *Adam,* (Gods peace be with him) after God had descended from Paradice, and been merciful to him after his Sin, was by God himself appointed King of the Earth, and Mankind descended of his Race. He was the first that Prayed to God, Fasted, and knew how to Read and Write. He was Beardless and Hairless, comely and well made. There was afterwards sent him one and twenty pages of Writings; then he dyed aged nine hundred and fifty years. His life should have been a thousand years but he bestowed fifty of them on his Son *David.* His Successor and Legatee was his Son *Seth,* to whom the Prophecy remained, and to whose Children continued the Prophecy, with the true Religion and the Superintendency of Divine Laws. God afterwards sent *Seth* twenty nine sheets. He liv'd on the Mountain and *Cabel* built in the bottom of the Valley. *Seth* lived nine hundred and twelve years, and had for Successor his Son *Enos,* who lived nine hundred and fifty years, and appointed for his

Successor after his death his Son *Cainan,* in whose favour he made his last Will, and afterwards distributed the Earth among the Sons of his Sons. *Cainan* died aged nine hundred and twenty years, and made his last Testament in favour of his Son *Mahalel.* In his time the square Temple was built. He died aged nine hundred seventy five years, and appointed for Successor his Son *Jared,* whom he taught all the Sciences, and told all that was to happen in the World. He considered the Stars, and read the Book of the secrets of the Kingdom, which was sent from Heaven to *Adam:* then he had to his son *Enoch,* who is *Edrisus,* Gods peace be with him. There was then King in the World *Mechavel* the son of *Cabel.* The Devil (Gods curse with him) went to him, seduced him by his deceits, and made him fall into errour; then he told him that there was born to *Jared* the son of *Mahalel* a son who should be an enemy to theie Gods, and come to great reputation. Whereto *Jared* answered, "Canst not thou destroy him?" "I'le endeavour to do it," said the Devil. Whereupon God gave *Edrisus* (Gods peace be with him) Angels to guard him from the Devil, and from his Progeny and Artifices. When he was grown up to adolescency, his Father made him Guardian of the Temple, and taught him the sheets of *Seth* and *Adam,* Gods peace be with them. He was very diligent in the reading and studying of them, and in observing the precepts thereof. Being come to forty years of age, God gave him the gift of Prophecy, and sent him from Heaven thirty sheets. His Father made him his Successor by Will, gave him the Sciences he was possess'd of, and sent him to King *Darael,* whom he taught Writing and Astrology. For he is the first who writ in the *Syriac* after *Seth,* and who described the state of the Stars. The Nations of Writing affirm he was the first who made Slaves and Servants, and establish'd Weights and Measures. He led Captive the Children of *Cabel;* he was skilled in Medicine and the Astronomical Tables, according to a supputation different from the *Indian.* God shewed him after he had prayed for it the sublime Figures. Spirits spoke to him; he knew the names of the Ascent and Descent, and Ascended and Descended, and turned the Sphere, and knew the significations of the Stars, and all that was to happen, and graved all Sciences upon Stones and upon Bricks. He had a long adventure with the Angel of Death, which it would be too long for us to relate. To speak briefly of him, he died, and God raised him up again; he saw Hell, and entered into Paradice, where he still is, being not come out of it.

They relate (says the Author, Gods mercy on him) that King *Mechavel* sent to desire *Jared* to send *Edrisus* to him, for he desired to see him. But he would by no means do it, whereupon *Mechavel* sent an Army against him, which yet could not come at him, in regard his Uncles, and all the progeny of *Seth,* secured him against it; for after *Seth* there was no other Prophet but *Edrisus. Jared* died, aged 750 years. *Edrisus* was called *Edrisus* (that is, *Reader)* because he had much read and studied the sheets. He was raised up into Paradise at the complete age of 300 years; God grant him peace and mercy. He was also called *Hermes,* which is the name of *Mercury.* He taught *Sabi* to write, and after *Edrisus* all who could write were called *Sabi.* He it was who foretold the coming of the Deluge, and the destruction of the world by water, which was to come over the Earth. *Edrisus* (before he was raised up) had made his Will in favour of his Son *Matusalech,* and had put the sheets into his hands. He had also recommended *Sabi* to assist him. *Sabi* was a man taught by *Edrisus,* and one who had made a great progress in the Sciences. They say *Edrisus* was the first who ordered the waging of war for the Faith; and that he did it himself against the sons of *Cabel. Matusalech* lived 932 years, after which the Testament passed to *Malec* his Son, who took possession of the sheets, and joyned the Sciences together. He confederated with the Children of his father, and assembled them together, and hindred their holding any correspondence with the children of *Cabel.* 'Twas he who saw as it were a Fire issuing out of his mouth, and burning the world; after which he had to his Son the Prophet *Noah,* Gods peace and mercy be with him; *Darmasel* (the Son of *Mechavel,* the Son of *Enoch,* the Son of *Gabod,* the Son of *Cabel,* the Son of *Adam,* Gods peace be with him) then reigning. This *Darmasel* had lifted up himself, and was grown great, and had subdued Kings, which had happened because the Devil (whom God curse) had called him

King *Darmasel.*

to the worship of the Stars, and to the Religion of the *Sabaeans;* insomuch that he had made Idols, and had built Temples to them, wherein he served them. They say no man got out of the bowels of the Earth so many Precious stones, Pearls, and other Minerals, as this King did. He was very severe to the Prophet of God *Noah,* and endeavoured much to do him harm; but God prevented him, and preserved the Prophet. *Darmasel* had lived 300 years when God sent *Noah,* who was then 150 years of age. He lived in his Nation according to what God had revealed to him 1000 years wanting 50; then he lived after the Deluge 200 years. He was the first Prophet that came after *Edrisus,* to whom God grant peace. His Law was to profess the Unity of God, to pray, to pay the Sacred Tribute, to observe Abstinence, and to fight in the way of God against the Children of *Cabel.* After that he called his Nation to God, and made them fear his chastisements. But they began presently to ill-treat him. Yet was it long ere they discovered his enterprise to King *Darmasel,* during which *Noah* was continually in the houses of their Idols and in their Temples. And when he said unto them, "My Friends, say there is no other God then the true God, and that I am his Servant and Apostle."

They put their fingers into their Ears, and their Heads into their Mantles, so displeasing was the discourse to them. Then when he came to say, "there is no other God then the true God," the Idols fell down with their faces to the ground; and then the People fell upon him and beat him till he fell down. After that King *Darmasel* heard of his carriage, and ordered him to be brought into his presence, accompanied by his own people, who held a Ponyard to his Throat, and to whom the King spoke thus: "Is this he who you say speaks reproachfully of the Gods, and would destroy Religion?"

"Yea," replyed they. Then he said to *Noah;*

"O *Noah,* what do they here tell me of thee, that thou opposest my Religion, and what thy Fathers Children believe? what Magick is this whereby thou hast made the Idols tumble out of their places? who taught thee this Doctrine? Great King, replyed *Noah,* were they Gods as you imagine, my discourses could not hurt them, and they would not have fallen out of their places. For my part, I am the Servant of God and his Apostle. Honour the true God, and imagine nothing equal to him, for he sees you."

Thereupon *Darmasel* put *Noah* into Prison till the Feast of the Idols came, to the end he should offer Sacrifice to them. He also caused the Idols to be returned into their places on their Thrones, and made Oblations to them. Then when the time of the Idol-Feast drew near, he commanded a Herald to assemble all the the People, that they might see what he did to *Noah*. Then *Noah* implored the assistance of God against him, and he was immediately troubled with a great Head-ach and a Phrensie, which continu'd a week, after which he died. He was put into a golden Coffin, wherewith a Procession was made in the Temple of the Idols, his Subjects weeping about him, and cursing and railing at *Noah*. Then they carried him (I mean the King) into the Pyramids, and disposed him into a Tomb which had been prepared for him. He had appointed his Son to be King after him. He brought *Noah* out of Prison, esteeming him a distracted person, and forbid under great penalties, his relapsing into the faults wherewith he was charged. *Noah,* Gods mercy to him, expected till the day of one of their great Festivals, on which they assembled themselves to serve their Idols. He then came to them and said thus, "Say there is no other God then the true God, and that I am his Servant and Apostle."

With those words the Idols fell down of all sides, and the people fell upon *Noah,* cruelly beating him, making several wounds in his head, and dragging him along the ground with his Face downwards. Then the Heavens and the Earth, the Mountains and the Seas cryed vengeance to God, saying, "O Lord, do you not see the cruel treatment made to your Prophet *Noah?*"

The Almighty and All-good God made them sensible that that cruelty was exercised on himself, that he would punish those Rebels, and do right to *Noah.* They afterwards carried *Noah* before the King, who spoke thus to him, "Have not I already pardoned thee, and opened my Fathers Prisons, conditionally thou shouldst not return to thy faults?" "I am (replied *Noah)* a Servant, who does what he is commanded." "Who hath given thee that command?" said the King. "My God," replyed *Noah.* "Who is that God?" said the King. "The Lord of the Heavens and the Earth," said *Noah,* "the Lord of all Creatures." "And what hath he commanded thee?" said the King. "He hath commanded me (replyed *Noah)* to call you to his service, and he commands you and your Subjects to forsake the Worship of Idols, and to follow the ordinances of Prayer, payment of the Sacred Tribute, and the observance of Fasting." "And if we do it not," said the King, "what will be the issue?" "If he please (replied *Noah)* he will immediately destroy you; and if he please he will give you time to reflect on your ways till a certain term." "Let thy God alone (said the King) and what he desires of us, and do thou thy self give over importuning us." "How can I give over (replied *Noah)* when I am a Servant who does what is commanded him, and cannot disobey his All-good and Almighty Master?"

Then the King (says the Author) caused *Noah* to be imprisoned, to make an oblation of him to the Idols, as his Father had done before. Presently after, *Saudib* who was a powerful Lord and a Priest, rebelled against the King, and attempted to deprive him of his Crown. The Wars which the King was engaged in against him diverted him from thinking on the business of the Prophet of God *Noah,* and obliged him to put him out of Prison, till he had the leisure to have him brought before him. He afterwards agreed with *Saudib,* by granting him a portion of the upper part of *Egypt,* and return'd to his Royal Palace. The Devil (Gods curse on him) soon began to sollicit him to put the Prophet of God *Noah* to death, but Almighty God diverted him, so that the affaires of *Noah* were in different postures. The Son of *Darmasel* sent thereupon to all the Kings of the Earth, desiring them to send him all the Priests and Doctors, that they might dispute against *Noah.* They came to him from all parts, and disputed against the Prophet; but he baffled them all. Among others came to him the *Egyptian* Priest *Philemon,* of whom we have already spoken, God shew him mercy. He disputed against him, and *Philemon* acknowledged the Unity of God, who directed him so that he became faithful, and embarqued with *Noah* in the Ship. After that God revealed his will to *Noah* in these terms: "*Make the Ark,*" and the rest of the Verse. "How shall I

The Ark. make it?" said *Noah*. Then *Gabriel* came to him, and shew'd him the Model of it, ordering him to give him the Figure of a *Gondola* of glass. He was ten years a building of it, and he made it of the *Indian Plane* Tree, a hundred Cubits in length, according to the measure of his time, and fifty Cubits in height, and divided it into three Stories. The people of his Countrey in the mean time pass'd by him, and laughed and scoffed at what he did. Some brought to him their little Children, and charged them to beware of him. And sometimes the Children seeing him, endeavoured to hurt and disturb him. When *Noah* had compleated the Ship, he made the entrance on the side, and it continued lying on the ground seven Moneths, till they had offered up to their Idols three companies of those who had believed *Noah*. Then was the Decree of their chastisement confirmed, and God commanded *Noah* to put into the Ship two pairs of every species.

"Whence shall I be able to get all that?" said *Noah*. Immediately God commanded the four Winds to bring together about him all he had ordered to be put into the Ark; which they did. He took in at the first door the Wild and Tame Beasts, the Reptiles and the Birds; at the second (which was that of the middle) he took in Meat and Drink, and the Body of *Adam*, which was in a Shrine. Then he entered himself at the highest door with his children, and those who had believed in him. Relations agree not about the number of the Faithful who entered into the Ark; most affirm they were forty Men, and forty Women. When *Noah* and his Companions were got into the Ship, the news of it came to the King, who began to laugh at it, saying, "Where is the water on which that Vessel is to Sail?" They knew well enough that the Deluge was to come, but had no notice of the time of its coming, that the will of God might be fulfilled upon them. Upon that *Mechavel* the Son of *Darmasel* got on Horseback, with a party of his People, and went first to the Temple of his Idols, where he stayed a while, then went towards the place where the Ship was, with an intention to fire it. Being come near it he call'd *Noah* with a loud voice, and *Noah* having answered him, "Where (said he) is the water which is to bear thee in this Ship?" "It will be immediately with you," replied *Noah,* "before you go out of this place." "Come down (O *Noah)*" said the King, "and also those who are with thee." "O unhappy Man!" said *Noah,* "turn to God, for behold his Chastisements are ready to fall upon you."

These words incensed the King, so that he commanded fire to be cast into the Ship, upon him and upon his Companions. But immediately there comes a Messenger in great haste, telling him for news that a Woman heating the Oven to bake her Bread, water rush'd out of it as out of a great Torrent.

"Unfortunate Man!" replied the King; "how could water come out of a hot Oven?" "Unfortunate King!" replied *Noah;* "'tis one of the signs of my Lords wrath, which is descending on you and yours, according to what he hath revealed to me to threaten you withall. Another sign of the same thing is, that the Earth is going to shake and to stagger, that the water is going to overflow it on all sides, and that it is going to spring up under the Horse's feet on which you are mounted, even in the place where you now are."

Immediately the King was obliged to put back his Horse from the place where he was, seeing the water springing up under his Feet by the permission of God.

The Deluge.

As soon as he was got to another place, behold his Messengers returning to him, tell him that the water was very much risen and augmented, which forc'd him to a sudden departure, to return with all speed to his Castle, that he might take his Servants and his Children, and dispose them into the Fortresses which he had prepared on the tops of the Mountains, and where he had put in provisions as much as he imagin'd would be necessary. But presently the Earth began to open, and the Feet of the Horses to enter into it, so that they could not get them out, which obliged them to get off, and to leave them there. In like manner the doors of Heaven were opened and let fall a great Rain, as if water had been poured out of great Earthen Pots, so that the waters overtook them ere they could recover the Mountains, and hindered their getting up to them. They justled and thrust one another, and knew not which side to turn by reason of the violence of the Thunder and Lightning, and the greatness of the evil which was come upon them. The Women carried their Children at their backs, then when the water was come up to their mouths they cast them under their feet, and endeavoured to save themselves. Had God been disposed to have compassion on the Unbelievers, he would have been merciful to the Mother and the Child. One of *Noah's* Sons was with the King, the Son of *Darmasel,* when he came to fire the Ship. His Father cried out to him, "O my dear Son, Embarque thy self with us. I will retire (said he) into a Mountain, which shall secure me from the water. *Noah* answered him according to what God had taught him, it is onely the mercy of God which can this day preserve any body from the chastisements."

He was destined misery and destruction, and he was one of those who were drowned. The water rose above the Earth 40 Cubits, and above the Mountains 40 Cubits. All that was upon the face of the Earth perished, the Markings and Signs therefore were defaced; by the permission of God there remained only the Ark and those within. Those who adore the Stars affirm nevertheless that there remained some places upon the Earth which the waters of the Deluge reached not: but the *Mussulmans* deny it. The *Persians* (whom God cursed) say, the History of the Deluge is not true, and make no mention of the Prophecy of *Noah,* in regard they are *Magi* by Religion, and adore the Fire. The *Indians* affirm in like manner that there happened nothing of it in their Countrey, and so also the Inhabitants of the Maritime Countries and of most of the *Indian* Islands They say the Ark continued on the water six Moneths, that it Sail'd by all the Countries of the Earth, in the East, and in the West, and that one week it compass'd about the place of the square Temple. They had with them a large Sea-Pearl put on a Thread, by means whereof they in the Ship distinguished between Day and Night, and the hours of Prayer. They had also their Cock which Crew, to call up the People to Divine Service. It is written in the Law of *Moses,* that God swore by himself that he would not punish any Nation by the Deluge after the Nation of *Noah.*

Different opinions of the Deluge.

The History of *Noah*, according to an Ancient Book found by the Author.

I found (says the Author of this Book, *Murtadi* the Son of *Gaphiphus*, on whom God have mercy) in a Book (the greatest part whereof was torn out) the History of *Noah*, with considerable Additions and Augmentations, which I will fully set down here, to the end this Book may want no advantage which may raise its value with those who shall read it, or hear it read, with the direction and assistance of God. These Augmentations then relate, that the Patriarch, the Father of *Noah*, (Gods peace be with him) dreamt that he saw issuing out of his Mouth a fire, which burnt the whole Terrestrial World. He thereupon awaked much astonished. Some days after he dreamt again, that he was upon a Tree in the midst of a great Sea without Shores, which also astonish'd him very much. After that there being born to him a Son, the Prophet of God *Noah*, the good tidings of it spread over the whole Earth; and the Priest *Galoumas* related it immediately to *Mechavel* the Son of *Darmasel*, assuring him further that the Terrestrial world should perish in his time, that is, in the time of *Noah*, whose life was to be very long. The Priests knew also by their Sciences, that there would happen a Deluge, which should drown the Earth and its Inhabitants; but they always hoped to secure themselves from what should happen with King *Darmasel*. The King therefore commanded that there should be strong Castles built on the tops of the Mountains, that they might retire thither and be safe as they imagined. They built seven Castles of that kind, according to the number of their Idols, whereof they gave them the names, and graved thereon their Sciences. After that *Noah* being grown up, (God grant him peace and mercy) God sent him to them for an Apostle, and there happen'd to him what God himself relates in his Book. *Noah* was of delicate complexion, his Head was somewhat long, his Arms very large, as also his Leggs, his Thighs very fleshy, his Beard long and broad: he was large and thick. He was the first Prophet that came after *Edrisus*, and he is numbered among the famous Envoys for their constancy and resolution. He liv'd 1250 years. The Philosophers will not have him live so long, as differing among themselves about long lives. His law prescribed the profession of the Unity of God, and the Sacred Combat against those who opposed the establishment of his Religion, commanding the good and forbidding the evil, ordered the following of things permitted, and the avoiding of things forbidden, and the observance of purity and cleanliness. Almighty God had commanded him to induce his Nation to the proefession of his Unity, to mind them of the good things they had received of him, and to raise in them a fear of his indignation. The History relates, that *Noah* was born in the Reign of *Mechavel,* the Son of *Darmasel,* and that being two hundred years of age *Mechavel* died, and had for Successor his son *Darmasel,* who was much addicted to the worship of the Idols, exalting them as much as lay in his power, and commanding the People to serve them well. In the mean time *Noah* began to Preach the Religion of Almighty God, going through the Market-places, the Assemblies, the Temples, the Inns, and calling the people to God. They kept his Preaching secret, and discovered nothing of it to King *Darmasel,* till such time as his enterprize having been observed, Men bewared of him, and the King heard of him. They say that *Mechavel* (God curse him) imprisoned *Noah* 3 years before he died; and that after his death his son *Darmasel* (who was his Successor) brought *Noah* out of Prison, and commanded him to forbear corrupting Religion, and exclaming against the Gods. There was among them for their seven great Idols a Feast which they celebrated every year, during which they assembled to offer Sacrifices, and make Processions about the Idols. The time of that Feast being come, which is also the Feast of *Jagoth,* the people came together from all parts, and then *Noah* came to that Assembly, and having pass'd through the midst of the People, and cry'd with a loud voice; O Friends, say as I do; There is no other God then the great God. The people put their fingers into their Ears, and their Heads into their garments, but the Idols fell at *Noah*'s cry; which obliged the men to fall upon him, and to beat him cruelly, giving him several wounds in the head, then dragging him along the ground, with his face towards the Kings Palace, into which they made him enter, and brought him before him.

"Have not I done thee a favour (said the King) in taking thee out of Prison, though thou hast spoken against our Religion, rail'd at our Gods, and forsaken the footsteps of thy Fathers and Grand-fathers? Mean time thou comest again to exercise thy Magick against the Gods, so as thou hast made them to fall from their thrones, torn from their stations, and the places of their honour and their glory. What hath forc'd thee to this extremity?" "If these Idols (replied *Noah*) were Gods as you imagine, they would not have fallen at my voice. Fear God, unhappy Prince; turn to him, and believe nothing equal to him; for he sees you." "Who is he (said the King) who has made thee so confident as to speak to me in these terms? I will sacrifice thy Bloud to the Idols."

He thereupon commanded him to be kept in prison till the day of the Feast of *Jagoth,* that he might be sacrificed to him; and that the Idols might at the same time be exalted to their thrones. But he saw afterwards a Dream which startled him, and obliged him to order *Noah* to be put out of prison, giving out among the people that he was distracted.

Noah being afterwards 500 years of age, had his son *Sem,* and after him *Cham,* and after him *Jam,* then *Japhet.* Their mother was named *Noubahe,* the Daughter of *Enos,* the son of *Enoch. Noah* was afterwards a long time preaching to his Nation, yet could convert to the profession of the Unity of God but a small company of the meaner sort of people; wherefore they made this reproach to him, according to what God himself said to him, *"Thou hast been followed by the dregs of the people." Noah* was a Carpenter, and those who believed in him were of his own profession. He spent afterwards three Ages in preaching always to the people the Religion of Almighty God, without other effect save that they grew the more impious and insolent. Nay, they kill'd some of those who believed in him, and rifled their houses; and then God revealed to him, that of his Nation there would be no other Believers save onely those who had already embraced the Faith. *Noah* despairing of their Conversion began to pray to God against them, and to say, *"O my Lord, suffer not upon earth any habitation of the Unbelievers."* Then Almighty God commanded him to build

Noah's Wife.

The time from *Adam* to the Deluge.

the Ship; then he smote them with Sterility, as well to the Fruits of the earth, as the Procreation of children, making their women unable to bring forth, and in like manner the Females of their Cattel incapable of generation, and withdrawing his benedictions from their Orchards and Agriculture. They invoked their Idols, but it did bestead them nothing with God. Then *Noah* began to build the Ship, and spent three years in cutting down *Indian* Plane-trees and polishing them, in making Nails and Pins, and providing whatever was necessary; then he set it together in the moneth of *Regebe*. Those of his Nation would needs pass by him as he was at work, laughing and making sport at him. After he had finished it, God commanded him to put into it two pairs of every *species*. Those who embarqued with him of the sons of *Adam* and his own were *Sem, Cham,* and *Japhet,* and the others who belonged to him and were of his family. The Angels brought to him *Adams* Shrine, which was in the Countrey of *Tehama,* which is the Septentrional Territory of *Meca.* There was also with him in the Ark the *Egyptian* Priest *Philemon,* with his family and his daughters. The rest were of the children of his Father, and of his Grandfather *Edrisus.* After the chastisement was completed by the destruction of the Inhabitants of the Earth, that the Heaven had given a check to the Rains, that the Earth by the permission of her Lord had drunk up the waters, and that the Ark rested on Mount *Gedis,* they went out and built a City, which they called *The Match of Fourscore,* and which is at this day famous in its place, under the name of *Themanine,* which signifies *Fourscore*. They say that the several Nations, though they were not ignorant of the Deluge, and that they knew well enough it was to come, yet could not learn of their Priests precisely the time of its coming; because it was the will of the Almighty and All-good God to punish them. The Mountains cast stones at them, and they knew not which way to turn to avoid the falling of the Rain and the Stones. They say also that the water which fell was hot and corrupted, as if it had come out of a boiling Pool of Sand. Some affirm, that the Ship continued on the water a hundred and fifty days; others, that it continued

11 Moneths; God knows how it was. Some affirm also that the Deluge happen'd in the Moneth of *Regebe,* and that the Ark nested on Mount *Geudis* the tenth day of the Moneth of *Mucharram.* There were between the descent of *Adam* and the Deluge two thousand one hundred fifty six years. When God would restore the Earth to a good condition, he sent a wind upon the water which dry'd it, and put a stop to the Springs. The ordinary light return'd to the World, and the Sun and the Moon, and the Night, and the Day. Forty days after God commanded *Noah* to open the Ark. He opened it, and let out the Raven to see how low the water was. The Raven went out, and stayed to feed on the Carrions of the dead, and returned no more. Whereupon *Noah* made imprecations against her, that she might always be a Stranger, and never a domestick Bird, and that it should feed on Carrions. Then he let out the Dove after her. She soon return'd with her feet dy'd with the slime of the Earth, which was grown hot. Wherefore *Noah* prayed God to preserve her swiftness to her, and that she might be a domestick Bird, and belov'd of Men. He pray'd him also to give her patience to endure the loss of her young ones, and gave her his benediction; her feet have been red from that very time. He let her go seven days after, and she return'd bringing an Olive-leaf in her Beak; and told him for news, that there was not remaining on the surface of the Earth any Tree but the Olive-tree. They say, the Earth was dry the 27th. day of the 11th. Moneth of the year. After that God revealed to *Noah,* that he should let out the Beasts and the Reptiles out of the Ark. *Noah* cry'd out so violently at it, that he fell into a Feaver.

They say, those who were in the Ark were incommodated with the dung of the Creatures, which oblig'd *Noah* to give a cuff o' th' Ear to the Elephant, by vertue of

The Elephant and Lion in the Ark.

which cuff the Elephant sneez'd and cast out a Hog, which took away that ordure. They say also that the Rats troubling them, *Noah* gave a box o' th' Ear to the Lion, who sneez'd out a Cat, which devour'd the Rats. Others say these stories were invented for pleasure sake, and that they are not of faith, as having no grounds. *Noah* came afterwards out of the

Ark with his four Sons, *Sem, Cham, Japhet,* and *Jacheton,* which is he whom God gave him in the Ship. Then God said thus to them; "Multiply, fill the Earth, and cultivate it; I give you my benediction, and take my curse from the Earth, permitting it to bring forth its good things, its fruits and productions." Then he added speaking to them; "Eat that which is permitted and good, and shun what is impure, as Beasts sacrific'd to Idols, or naturally dead, and Swine's Flesh, and whatever hath been Sacrific'd to any other then God. Kill no man, for God forbids the doing of it, unless it be by the way of Justice."

It is written in the Law of *Moses,* that after they were come out of the Ark and settled in the Earth, God spake thus to them; "Multiply and fill the Earth, let the Beasts of it fear and respect you, and all the Fowls in the Air, and all the Fish in the Sea."

In the great *Alcoran* it is spoken of this in these terms; "Then it was said to him, O Noah, *descend out of the Ark in peace on our part,*" and the rest of the Verse. Then *Noah* ordered them to build every one a Habitation, whereupon they built fourscore of them in the City, which is to this day called the City of *Themanine,* that is, *Fourscore.* They afterwards fell a Sowing and Planting of Trees. They had ready for that end the Seeds, the Corn, and the Fruit, which had been put up in the Ship; there was onely the Vine, that is the Tree which bears Grapes, which *Noah* wanted and could not find. Whereupon *Gabriel* told him that the Devil had stolen it away, as having some part in it. *Noah* thereupon sent for him, and when he was present he said to him; "O cursed Spirit, why hast thou done this? Because I have part in it, said the Devil. Divide it then between you," said *Gabriel.* "I am content" said *Noah;* "I resign him the fourth part of it." "'Tis not enough for him," said *Gabriel.* "Well," said *Noah,* "I will take one half, let him take the other." "It is not yet enough, said *Gabriel;* but he must have two thirds of it, and thou one. When therefore the juice of it shall have boyl'd over the fire, till two thirds thereof be consum'd, thou shalt be allow'd the use of the rest; and in like manner the Grape as well new as dry, and

What part the Devil hath in the Vine.

the Viniger. As to the surplusage which may inebriate, it is forbidden thee and thy posterity; thou art not to expect any part thereof from the Devil, nor to commence any action against him for it."

Then the Devil (God hinder him from doing harm) said thus to *Noah*, (Gods peace be with him;) "I am oblig'd to you for the great kindness you have done me, and for which I shall not be ungrateful. O *Noah*, beware of Envy, Intemperance, Avarice, and Impatience. For Envy enclin'd me to make God incensed against me, and was the cause of my banishment out of Paradice. Intemperance made your Father *Adam* transgress the Commandment of his Lord, and eat the fruit of the Tree. Avarice made *Cabel* kill his Brother *Abel*: And Impatience brought you to make imprecations against your Nation, which caused God to bring destruction on all, and hath given a relaxation of the pains I took to deceive them."

Then *Noah* caused the Shrine wherein *Adams* body was, to be brought into the Cave of Old Age at *Meca*, and left it there. The History relates, that when *Noah* took the Scorpion and the Serpent into the Ship with him, he pray'd his Almighty and All-good Lord, to take away their venom from them, which was

The Scorpion and the Serpent.

granted. When therefore he put them out of it they spoke thus to him: "O Prophet of God, pray your Lord for us, that he would restore us our venom, and that we may make our advantage thereof against our enemies, and by means thereof defend our selves against those who would injure us. We promise you in requital, and in the name of God we grant, that whoever shall every day and every night pronounce these words, *God grant peace to* Noah *for ever,* we will not come near him, and will do him no hurt."

Noah pray'd to his Lord, and he order'd the making of that agreement, and that security to be taken of them: and after he had done it God restored to them their venom, according to what he had ordain'd by his Providence, since no man can destroy what he has ordain'd, nor defer the execution of his Judgments. They say moreover that when the Chastisement was taken from the Inhabitants of the Earth, and that fair weather ha succeeded the Clouds, *Noah* look'd up on high, and that having observed the Rain-bow, he said thus; "What means this, O Lord?" And that God answer'd him, "This is an assurance for the Inhabitants of the Earth, that there shall be no more Deluge."

Kings of *Egypt* before the Deluge.

The Kings of *Egypt* who Reigned before the Deluge, (says the Author) and were *Coptites,* are *Craos* the Gyant, and his son *Tegares,* and his son *Mesram,* and his son *Gancam,* and his son *Gariac,* and his son *Louchanam,* and his son *Chasalim,* and his son *Harsal,* and his son *Jadousac,* and his son *Semrod,* and his son *Josedon,* and his son *Sariac,* and his son *Sahaloc,* and his son *Saurid* who built the Pyramids, and his son *Hargib,* and his son *Menaos,* and his son *Ecros.* After that the succession from Father to Son was interrupted which oblig'd the *Egyptians* to take for their King a certain man of the Royal House named *Ermelinos;* and after him *Pharaan,* who was the first who reigned insolently and tyrannically, and who gave the name to the *Pharaohs.* He was also the last of the Kings of *Egypt* before the Deluge.

Darmasel and Philemon.

The first of the Kings of *Egypt* after the Deluge was *Masar,* the son of *Mesraim,* (who is *Bansar*) the son of *Gham,* the son of *Noah,* to whom God grant peace and mercy. This *Masar* was son to the daughter of the Priest *Philemon,* who believed in *Noah.* For they say that *Pharaan* (the last of the Kings of *Egypt* before the Deluge) grew proud upon the earth, and treated his people insolently and tyrannically, taking away their goods, and committing Injustices, such as none had done before or after him; and shedding Mens bloud by his continual murthers. Nay, Kings themselves were afraid of him, and respected him. He it was who writ to *Darmasel* the son of *Mechavel* King of *Babylon,* and advised him to put *Noah* to death. *Darmasel* had already written to the Inhabitants of *Gueraca,* and of all the other Provinces, to know of them whether there were any other Gods besides the Idols; and had related to them the History of *Noah,* and the Religion which he preached, and how he incited them to the worship of one onely

God, different from those whom they adored. Every one of them had rejected this, and had advised him to put *Noah* to death. But after God had commanded *Noah* to build the Ark, *Pharaan* King of *Egypt* writ to *Darmasel,* exhorting him to fire it; which *Darmasel* thought to do, but at the same time the Prince of the Priests of *Egypt (Philemon)* gave him other advice; and writ to him that he counselled him to leave it as it was, in regard that if what that man said was true, that is, what *Noah* said, the King should embarque with those of his house, and then put *Noah* to death that he might be no more troubled with him. The Learned of *Egypt* knew well that the Deluge was to come, but knew not how great it was to be, nor how long it was to continue on the surface of the earth. The Priest *Philemon* dreamt as he slept, that he saw *Emsos* (which is the City of *Masre)* overturned upon its Inhabitants, and the Idols falling with their Noses to the ground; and that there descended from Heaven men armed with sharp pointed Instruments of Iron, wherewith they beat the people; and that he seemed to approach one of them, and spoke to him thus; "Why treat you the men after that manner?" "Because (replied he) they are ungrateful and irrespective towards their God, who hath created them, and gives them subsistence." "Is there no means for them to be saved?" said *Philemon.* "Yes," replied the other: "those who would be saved are onely to apply themselves to him who hath built the Ark."

Philemon awaked thereupon very much astonished. He had a wife and two children, a son and a daughter, and seven of his Disciples. He therefore settled his affairs, with an intention to go to *Noah,* Gods peace be with him. Then afterwards he saw another Dream; He seem'd to be in a green Medow, where there were white Birds which smell'd of Musk; and as he stood still to take a view of them, and to admire their beauty, one of them began to speak, saying to the rest; "Let us go, let us deliver the Believers." Whereupon *Philemon* said to him, "Who are those Believers?" "They are (replied the Bird) the men of the Ark."

He thereupon awaked very much astonished and affrighted, and related that to those of his House and his Disciples. Then he went and spoke to the King in these terms; "I have seen a Dream, according to which if it please Your Majesty to send me to *Darmasel* King of *Babylon*, I shall know what that man is who hath built a Ship in a dry Countrey. I will discourse with him, and dispute against him about this new Religion which he preacheth, and would introduce, and will inform my self of the truth of his pretensions; and I hope at length to turn him out of the way which he would have others to follow."

The King approved the design, and ordered him to depart. *Philemon* then left *Egypt*, with his Family and his Disciples, and travelled till he came to *Babylon*, and discoursed with *Noah*, Gods peace be with him, so as that he found what he said to be true, and believed in him, and followed his Religion. "When God will put a man into the right way (said *Noah*) no man can put him out of it."

Philemon continued with *Noah* ever after, and ceased not to serve him and his Children, and his Family, and his Disciples, till they imbarqued with him in the Ark.

Mean time *Pharaan* (God curse him) continued his divertisements, and remained in his errour, unworthily treating the people of *Egpyt*, and afflicting them by his Injustices and Murthers, which caused many Tumults and Spoils in the Countrey, and dearth of provisions, Men oppressing one another, and no body reproving vice. The Temples and the *Birbas* were lock'd up, and their doors full of dirt. The Deluge came upon them, and the Rain overwhelm'd them on Sunday the 24th. day of the Moneth, *Pharaan* being then drunk; so that he came not to himself till the water began to fasten on him. He started up of a sudden, and ran away as fast as he could; but his feet sunk into the ground, and he fell on his Face, and fell a roaring like a Bull, till the Unbeliever perish'd, he and all his Nation. Those who retired into some Cave or other secret place perished there also. The water cover'd the *Pyramids* to the end of the Quadrature. The marks of it are manifest to this day. After the Deluge the first who Reign'd in *Egypt* was *Masar*, the Son of *Bansar*, the Son of *Cham*, the Son of *Noah*. The *Mussulmans* who follow the Traditions affirm, that this *Masar* was the first King of *Egypt* after the Deluge, and that he became so, having been before designed for it by his Grandfather *Noah*, which happen'd upon this, that *Philemon* intreated *Noah* to have a particular affection for him, and for his Family and his Children, and spoke to him thus: "O Prophet of God, I am come to you out of desire I had to believe in God, and to follow your precepts; I have to that end forsaken my Countrey, and the place of my Birth, give me some Prerogative and Preheminence, which may cause me to be spoken of after I am." "What do you desire in order to that?" said *Noah*. "I desire (said *Philemon*) that you would joyn my Family to yours, and that you would take this my Daughter to be Wife to one of your Sons."

Noah took her and married her to *Mesraim*, the Son of *Cham*, to whom she bore a Son, whom his Grandfather *Philemon* named *Masar*. When *Noah* would afterwards divide the Earth amongst his Children, *Philemon* spoke to him in these terms; "O Prophet of God, send along with me this my Son, (meaning *Masar*) and permit me to bring him into my own Countrey, to shew him the Treasures of it, and to teach him the Sciences and remarkable things thereof."

Noah sent him along with him, accompanied by some of his own House. He was a delicate young man, and they travelled during the great heat of the Sun, so that when they came near the Land of *Egypt*, *Masar* made a kind of Arbour of the Boughs of Trees, at the place now called *Garisa*, that is to say, the *Arbour*, and covered it with the Grass he found on the ground. Near that place he afterwards built a City, which he called *Darsan*, that is to say, the Door of the Garden, about which they planted Trees, and sow'd the grounds, and made sweet smelling Orchards. Between *Darsan* and the Sea-side there were tilled Fields and Gardens, and well cultivated grounds. *Masar*'s people were mighty robust and valiant. They cut stones, and raised remarkable Buildings, and liv'd very much at ease for a long time. *Masar* married a Woman of the Race of the Priests, of whom he had a Son named *Coptim*, and he was the Father of all the *Coptites*. Afterwards at ninety years of age he married another Woman, and had by her Sons, *Coptarim* and *Asmomus*, and *Abribus*, who grew up and peopled the Land, and were prosperous therein. Their Cities were called from their names, and will be so call'd till the day of Judgment.

They say the number of those who accompanied *Masar* was thirty Men, and that they built a great City, which they called *Maca;* for *Maca* signifies thirty; and that it is the City of *Memphis*. *Philemon* afterwards discovered to them the Treasures of *Egypt,* made them understand the writing of the *Birbas,* opened the Pyramids for them, and taught them the Talismans of their gates, and the ways to be obey'd by the Spirits appointed over them. He shew'd them the Mines of Gold and Silver, and Topazes, and Turqueses, and Esnadosammes. He taught them the Art of handling white and black Marble and Jasper, whereof they made their Vessels and Instruments, and the Pillars of their habitations. He writ down for them the Operations of the Art, which he attributed to a Man of his house named *Moncatam,* who practised Chemistry upon Mount *Mactam.* They say the origin of the art of working Marble (as well White as Black) came from Chemistry; in as much as the waters and essences, which they distill and circulate by their artifices, passing through the earthen vessels, he compos'd for them the white stone in Sand and Glass, and made the hard red stone for them of a soft stone and red Arsnick, or Sandarack and Pitch: he kindled a fire thereon, and ordered them by his wisdom. He made Mills for them in the ground, and caused these materials to be put into them; then the stones came out figured after what manner they desired in all sorts of vessels. Nay, they say that the stones were soft with them from the break of day till the afternoon; and that they made what they would of them. *Philemon* taught them also to make Talismans; for there came out against them out of the Sea certain Creatures which threw down their Buildings, whereupon they made Talismans against those Creatures, and they never came afterwards. They built several Cities upon the *Roman* Sea, and among others that of *Racoda,* at the place where now *Alexandria* stands. They made in the midst of that City a little Turret upon pillars of Copper guilt, and set upon it a Mirrour consisting of a mixture of divers materials, in length and breadth five spans, and the Turret of the height of 100 Cubits according to their measure. When therefore any Enemy came against them, they made certain Opera-

Moncatam's Chemistry.

tions on the Mirrour, then they made the rays of it fall on the Enemy, so that they burnt him. This Turret and the Mirrour remained there till the Sea reach'd and destroyed them. The *Pharos* also of *Alexandria* had not been made but for a Mirrour that was upon it, and discovered those who came against them from the *Roman* Countrey. One of the *Roman* Emperours prevailed so far by his artifices and great expences, that he destroyed it. It was of white Marble well design'd, and well wrought. They relate (says the Author, to whom God be merciful) that God promised *Noah* (Gods peace be with him) to hearken to him in a prayer he should make for his son, and that he deferred that prayer till the next morning; at which time very early in the morning he was to call his son, and him of his sons who should readily answer him God would bless when he had prayed for him; and he who answered not should not have that benediction. The readiest to answer was *Sem,* wherefore he prayed God for him and his posterity: and the most backward to answer were *Cham* and *Japhet,* wherefore he prayed God against them. *Masar* the son of *Bansar,* the son of *Cham,* was an useful and serviceable Young man; for which reason *Noah* cherished him, and he was always with him, never leaving him. Having therefore heard the prayer which *Noah* had made against his Grandfather and his children, and the children of his children, he fell a weeping, and turned to *Noah,* and said thus to him; "O Great Grandfather, I have heard the Imprecations you have made against my Grandfather *Cham,* and against his children; and yet for my part I have been always obedient to you, and ready to serve you: Pray therefore unto God for me."

The *Pharaos* of *Alexandria.*

These words pleased *Noah,* and immediately he put his hand on his head, saying; "O great God, behold here one of my sons, who answered me when I have called him; bless him, him and his posterity, and divert from them weakness, and grief, and affliction; and give them generosity and valour, and drive away far from them trouble, care,

***Noah*'s Prayer for *Masar*.**

and displeasure. Arm the middle of their bodies with girdles of Steel; never let them be disabled to perform the Sacred voyage; give them for their habitation a Land whereof the air is pleasant, the waters sweet, and the pastures green; which may be the Mother of Nations, and the relief of Men; which may allure to it all sorts of persons, Citizens and Countrey-people, out of all the Plains and out of all the Mountains, both far and near; a Land that hath a River transcending all Rivers, whereof the History may be the most admirable of Histories; from which the Abysses of the Sea are derived, which divides the Desarts of Countries with its pregnant surges and swollen waves, from the remainder of Countries to the Metropolis of all other places; the chosen City, the Countrey of fair ways, through which the noble *Nile* flows with its excellent waters, on which the eye of the Almighty watches night and day, supplied with springs and fair waters; the Favourite of Heaven in all its parts, adorned with a River coming from Paradise, replenished with the favours of the Gratificator, and the mercies of the Merciful; where Plants sprout forth and thrive exceedingly, where there is abundance of all sorts of good things, and an afluence of all benedictions."

Masar's Tomb.

After that *Noah* prayed his Lord to subject the Land to *Masar* and his children, to sortifie them over it, and to make it submissive to them, to assist them to cultivate it, and to relieve the Prophets among them. *Noah* (Gods peace be with him) was heard in all this. When *Masar* (says the Author) was near death, he made his Will in favour of his son *Coptim.* He had before divided the Land among his children, and had given *Coptarim* all the Countrey which reaches from *Copta* to *Syene;* to *Asmoumus,* what is from *Asmon* to *Memphis;* and to *Abribus,* all the flat Countrey from about *Saram* and the Fennes, as far as beyond *Barca;* so that he was Lord also of *Afric* and the *Africans.* He recommended it to every one of his children to build himself a City in his Country; and enjoyn'd them all together (at the hour of his death) to make him a Cave in the earth, to pave it with white Emeralds, to dispose his Body into it; and to bury with him whatever there was in his Treasuries of Gold, Silver, and Precious Stones; and to write thereupon such names as might divert any from approaching it. They made a Cave 150 Cubits in length, and in the midst a place of Assembly wainscoated with Plates of Gold and Silver, having 4 Doors, and over every Door a Statue of Gold, wearing a Crown beset with Precious stones, and seated on a Throne of Gold, the feet whereof were of Topaze. They graved on the breast of each Statue great names, able to divert any from approaching them, and disposed the body of *Masar* into a Tomb of Marble covered with Plates of Gold, and writ upon it, *"Masar, the son of Bansar, the son of Cham, the son of Noah, died aged seven hundred years from the days of the Deluge. He died without ever having adored any Idol, not broken with old age, nor troubled with sickness, not having felt any evil or pain, nor afflicted with any sadness, care, or displeasure."* They fortified him also with the great Names of GOD, which never permit such as are fortified therewith to fall into contempt, or be oppressed. They swore moreover the greatest of all Oaths, that none should come near him, unless he were a King who had 7 of his sons Kings; and not any of them a servant, or slave, or poor, or necessitous, who followed the Religion of the King the just Judge, that is to say, the true God, and believed the Prophet of the Merciful, sent with the *Alcoran* to bring the World to the Faith in the last times. They also placed near him a thousand pieces of Topaze made round about him, and a thousand Statues of precious Stones of great value, and *Gernes* or great Vessels, containing the Sciences of the Divine Art, and the secret Drugs, and the admirable Talismans, and Ingots of gold in great heaps, like sand or stones. They cover'd that Cave with great stones and sand spread thereon, between two Mountains opposite one to the other.

Kings of *Egypt* after the Deluge.

The first King of *Egypt* who Reigned after the Deluge was *Masar,* the son of *Bansar,* the son of *Cham;* after him Reign'd his son *Coptim,* then his son *Coptarim,* then his son *Budesir,* then his son *Gadim,* then his son *Sedathe,* then his son *Mancaos,* then his son *Casaos,* then his son *Marbis,* then his son *Asmar,* then his son *Citin,* then his son *Elsabas,* then his son *Sa,* then his son *Malil,* then his son *Hadares*, then his son *Cheribas*, then his son *Calcan*, then his son *Totis*, who is he whom the *Arabians* call *The Just*. For this is the *Pharao* of *Egypt*, who had conversation with the Beloved of God *Abraham*, (Gods peace be with him) as also with *Mahumet*, and Mercy, and who by force would have taken away from him his Wife *Sara*, which happen'd thus: The Beloved of God, (Gods peace and mercy be with him) after God had destroy'd the cursed *Nimrod* his enemy, took his Journey out of the Land of *Gueraca*, and came to *Egypt*, accompany'd by his Wife *Sara*, (Gods peace be with her) and left *Lot* behind him in *Syria*. *Sara* was one of the most beautiful Women in the World; they say *Joseph* (Gods peace be with him) inherited her Beauty. *Abraham* therefore (says the Author) being come he and his wife into *Egypt*, the Guards who were at the City-gate having seen *Sara* admired her beauty, and went presently to give notice of it to King *Totis*, and said to him; There came into the City a man of the Eastern Countrey, accompany'd by a Woman the most beautiful and most handsom that can be seen. Immediately *Totis* sent for *Abraham*, and said to him, "Whence are you?" "Of *Gueraca*," reply'd *Abraham*. The King enquired further of him concerning his business, and he gave him an account thereof. Then he said to him, "What relation hath that woman to you?" "She is my Sister," said *Abraham*. Then the King said to his Visier, "Bid him bring her to me, that I may see her."

The History of *Abraham* and *Totis* King of *Egypt*.

That displeased *Abraham* very much, but it was not possible for him to disobey; yet he knew that God would not permit any dishonour to happen in his Family; he therefore said to *Sara*, "Go your ways to the King, but without fear or troubling your self, for you are under his tuition who hath created you, who will divert from you whatever you may be afraid of, and will assist both you and me with his favours." "But what would the King with me (said *Sara*) more then with you?" "I hope (said *Abraham*) it will be nothing but what is good, with the help of the Almighty."

They therefore conducted *Sara* to *Totis*'s Palace, accompany'd by *Abraham*. The King having seen her was surpriz'd with her beauty and behaviour, and said to *Abraham,* "What is this Woman to you?" "She is my Sister," reply'd *Abraham.* He meant his Sister in God, according to the Religion which he professed. Whereupon *Abraham*'s heart felt the ordinary sentiments of a jealous man; he wished he had never come into *Egypt.* Then he began to say, "O God, suffer not the Family of *Abraham* to be dishonoured." At which words the Veils and the Curtains were drawn before him, so that he saw *Sara* speaking to the King. The King put forth his hand to touch her, but she presently said to him, "If you put your hand on me you are undone." Accordingly even before the Kings hand was quite come to *Sara,* and had touched her, that hand shrunk up, all the Kings members shook, and Death presented it self on all sides. He continued immoveable, not able to stir, and spoke thus; "O Woman, deliver me from the evil that is fallen upon me, and go whither you will." "I will do it (said she) conditionally you do not renew your attempt against me." "I promise it," reply'd the King.

Whereupon she prayed God for him, and God delivered him from the evil which had happen'd to him. He recovered his health, and said, "Certainly he is a great Lord whom you adore; that is manifest." Then he enquir'd of her who *Abraham* was, and of what Religion.

He is the darling of God; (reply'd she) his Religion is the profession of the Unity of the Almighty, and he is my Husband. He told me (reply'd the King) that you were his Sister. He told you truth (said *Sara)* for I am his Sister in God, and so all who make profession of our Religion are our Brethren in God. Yours is a noble Religion, reply'd the King.

He afterwards sent *Sara* to his Daughter *Charoba.* That young Virgin was ingenious, handsom, and well-inclined, as much as could be wished; and therefore she made great account of *Sara,* took her into her affection, honoured her much, and gave her a very kind reception; nay, she sent her precious Stones of great value, and Money, and rich Garments. *Sara* brought all to *Abraham;* but he

Charoba, Totis's Daughter.

told her she should restore them, and that they needed them not. *Sara* therefore returned all to *Charoba,* who was much astonish'd at it, and acquainted her Father with it; who thereupon doubled the admiration which he had for the Beloved of God, seeing him refuse things which any other would have eagerly sought, having any means to obtain them. He therefore esteemed and honoured him much, and said to his daughter, "These are persons of good repute, who come out of a House full of purity and sincerity, and great prudence, and are not covetous of perishable goods. *Charoba,* do whatever you can imagine best to honour them."

Charoba afterwards bestowed on *Sara Agar,* who is the Mother of our Father *Ismael,* Gods peace be with him. As she gave her her, she said to her *Hacagare,* that is to say, *Behold thy recompence:* for which reason *Sara* call'd her *Agar.* She was a *Coptess* by Nation, and one of the handsomest young maids of her time, Gods peace be with her. After that the Beloved of God being resolved to return out of *Egypt* into *Syria, Charoba* provided for them several Baskets of Conserves, and other excellent things to eat, saying; *"This is onely for your better Provision by the way, and not to enrich you."* *Sara* told *Abraham* of it, who said, that as to that he would accept of it, and that there was no hurt in receiving it of the Princess. *Charoba* caused it to be loaden on Mules, and afterwards caused them to mount thereon, sending along with them some of her people to conduct them, and to wait on them, till they were got out of the Land of *Egypt.* Having travelled a good part of their Journey, *Abraham* said to *Sara,* "Give us to eat somewhat of that which the Princess of *Egypt* gave to you."

Sara set the Baskets before him, and he did eat thereof, he and those of his Company: but when they came to the last Basket, they found it full of several sorts of Jewels, and precious Stones, and Garments. Whereupon the Beloved of God said to *Sara,* "The Princess of *Egypt* hath deceived us, and hath carried her business so as that we have brought away of her goods. Great God, give her subtilty against those who will do her hurt, and strive with her for her Land; bless her in her

Abraham's Prayer for Charoba.

Countrey, and in her River; make that Countrey a place of safety and prosperity."

When the Beloved of God (said the Author) was come into *Syria*, he spent those Presents in Pious works, lodging Pilgrims, and making the Well which he ordered to be common. He also bought Flocks, which he design'd for Travellers, for the Poor and Necessitous, for Passengers, for the Lame. God gave them his benediction, and caused them to multiply. *Sara* put up a little thereof for two Children which she had. *Totis* King of *Egypt* lived after that till such time as *Agar* sent to him out of the Countrey of *Meca*, to acquaint him that she was in a barren Land, that she had a famous and renowned Son, and that there were about her a great number of *Arabians*, whom the barrenness of the Countrey had quite chang'd, and that she intreated him to relieve her with some provisions. To that end *Totis* caused a Chanel to be made in the Eastern part of *Egypt*, at the foot of the Mountain, and brought into it the water of the *Nile*, so that it might carry Vessels into the salt Sea, which is the Chanel of the Red Sea. By that way he caused Wheat to be sent to *Agar*, as also all sorts of Corn, and Presents. They went by water as far as *Gedde*, and thence they were carried to *Meca* on the backs of Beasts. By these means God long preserved alive the Inhabitants of *Meca*, which obliged them to call that King *The Just*, as having performed the promise he had made them, and given great testimonies of the affection he had for them. They say also that *Agar*, after her delivery of *Ismael*, (Gods peace be with him) sent to *Charoba* to acquaint her with the news of her Lying-in; whereat she was very glad, and sent her abundance of Jewels, and Gold, and *Egyptian* Linen to dress her Son withall. Out of one part of these Presents she established a Porter in the square Temple. Nay, they say that all the Ornaments of the square Temple, which were put into it at that time came from *Egypt*, Presents from *Totis* and his daughter *Charoba*.

The History relates, that *Totis* desired the Well-beloved of God to desire of God his benediction for his Countrey. *Abraham* therefore prayed God for the Inhabitants of *Egypt*, and gave his benediction to its *Nile*, and assured *Totis* that his posterity should reign there, and be Masters thereof to the last times age after age. They relate that *Totis* was the first called *Pharao* in *Egypt*, because he was cruel and bloudy, and put many people to death, even of his nearest Relations, and those of his own House, and that out of the envy he bore them, fearing the Crown should be taken away from his daughter after his death, for he had no other children. She was of a milde and good disposition, and a great Wit. She always endeavoured to prevent the shedding of bloud, but could not prevail: wheresore she was at last afraid they would take away the Crown from him, seeing him extremely hated by all people, which made her resolve to dispatch him by poison, after he had reigned 70 years. *Totis* being dead, the people could not agree upon whom they were to make King in his stead. Some said they should take in some of the Progeny of *Abribus*, because they had anciently reigned: but one of the Visiers began to speak thus; "My Friends, *Charoba* is a woman of understanding: besides, she has delivered you from this Tyrant, out of the extraordinary kindness she had for you. Moreover, the good man that came from *Syria* and his wife also have given her their benedictions. If you give the Crown to any other, you will repent you of it."

Charoba poisoning her Father reigns after him.

The people inclined to this advice, and thought that counsel good. Most of the Grandees of *Egypt* followed it; so that *Charoba* did her work, and that Visier made her Queen. After that she sate in the Royal Throne, made great Liberalities, and promised much happiness to the people. She honoured the Souldiery, gave them great gifts, and doubled their Pay. She in like manner honoured the Priests and the Sages, and the chiefest among the people; made great account of the Magicians, and heightned their rank, and caused the Temples to be rebuilt and enlarged. She was afterwards many years Queen of *Egypt* by the benediction of *Abraham*, (Gods peace be with him) and not attaqued by any Enemy who was not presently overcome and subdued by her with the assistance of God.

The History of *Gebirus* and *Charoba*.

Gebirus the *Metapheguian* came to give her a visit: he encamped in the Land of *Balca*, and had a Brother named *Gebrim*, taking his name from him: they were two Giants of the remnant of the *Gadites*. When *Gebirus* sate down on the ground upon the sand, those who were in the midst of the Sea saw him. He had a Kive 30 Cubits about, which being filled full of meat for him he eat up all; then they filled it with wine, and he drank it off. He happened to have the plague in his body, which put him to great pain, increasing every day; whereupon his Physicians advised him to send some of his people about the Countrey to find out for him a soil, whereof the Air and Waters were agreeable to his Temperament. These gave him an account of the Countrey of *Egypt*, which obliged him to come thither, after he had drawn up his Forces together, and distributed Money and Arms among them. He brought along with him 4000 *Gadites*, every one of whom carried a stone of the breadth of the *Nile* of *Egypt*. He travelled so long till he got near the Land of *Egypt*, and approched it at that part where the Queen was willing he should, for he did not contradict her in any thing, his design being to get her to marry him; and by that means make him King of *Egypt:* or (if she denied him) to dam up with the stones the course of the *Nile,* and turn it into another Countrey, and so make the *Egyptians* die of hunger and thirst. *Charoba* sent to him a Servant-maid she had, one who managed her affairs, a very subtile Wench, a great Enchantress, and a Cheat: she saw with him huge Bodies, which there was no means to overcome by fighting; wherefore she advised her Mistress not to engage into a war against him: "I shall endeavour rather (said she) to defeat him by some stratagem, and to carry the business so as that he may neither hurt you nor your Subjects."

After that she took along with her what was most pleasant in *Egypt,* Conserves, beautiful Garments, sweet Scents, Arms, Gold and Silver; and with all this desired permission to visit *Gebirus,* which was soon granted her. She presented to him all these Rarities, which he willingly received. Then she told him that the Queen of *Egypt* was in Love with him, and desirous to Marry him, and far from refusing so advantageous a Match. This news made him jocund, and put him into a good humour. He return'd her this answer; "Promise the Queen from me for a Marriage-gift what you please your self." "The Queen (reply'd she) needs not any thing of yours, since your affairs will hence forth be common; but she desires of you instead of a Marriage-present, that you cause a City to be built in her Land, on the side of the *Roman* Sea, that it may be an honorable mark to her to the end of the World; and that it may be a discovery of your power; and that you employ in the Building of it these Stones and these Pillars which you have brought with you to dam up the Chanel of the *Nile.*"

He granted her Request, and entered into the Land of *Egypt* with his Forces, and founded the City on the West-side, at the place where now *Alexandria* is; to that end encamping himself and his Army on the *Roman* Sea-side. *Charoba* sent him several sorts of Presents and Refreshments. *Alexandria* was then ruin'd, ever since the *Gadites* went out of *Egypt:* for it had been founded by *Sedad,* the Son of *Gad,* who had a design to bring thither whatever was most precious in all the quarters of the Earth, for he was the Monarch of the World East and West. But the Destroyer of Castles prevented him, I mean Death, which none can divert or avoid; yet were there some tracks of it as some affim. *Gebirus* caused to be brought thither the Stones, and the Pillars, and assembled the Artists and the Engineers.

Charoba sent him also a thousand Handy-craftsmen. He spent a long time in Building, so that his money was exhausted, and his people could do no more. For when they had built and made some advancement, as soon as the evening was come, while they took their rest in the night, they were astonish'd in the morning, that they could find no sign of what they had done. For there came out of the Sea certain people who took away all into the salt waters. *Gebirus* was extreamly troubled and afflicted thereat. *Charoba* sent him a thousand Goats or Sheep, which were milk'd for the Kings Kitchin. They were kept by a Shepherd belonging to *Gebirus,* of whom he had received that charge. This Shepherd led them out to graze, accompany'd by a great many other Shepherds, upon the Sea side.

The Nymph *Marina*.

One day this Shepherd (having put the Beasts into the custody of the other Shepherds, who obeyed him) being a beautiful person, and of a good Aspect and Stature, saw a fair young Lady issuing out of the Sea, which came towards him, and being come very near him saluted him; he return'd the salutation, and she began to speak to him with all imaginable courtesie and civility, and said to him; "Young man, would you wrestle with me for something which I should lay against you?" "What would you lay?" reply'd the Shepherd. "If you give me a fall (says the young Lady) I will be yours, and you shall dispose of me as you please; and if I give you a fall, I will have a beast out of your Flock." "Content," said the Shepherd; and thereupon he went towards her, and she came towards him. He began to wrestle with her, but she immediately flung him, and took a beast out of the Flock, which she carried away with her into the Sea. She came afterwards every evening, and did the like, so that the Shepherd was over head and ears in love with her. The Flock diminish'd, and the Shepherd himself pin'd away. One day King *Gebirus* passing by the Shepherd, found him sitting near his Flock very pensive, which obliged him to come nearer him, and to speak thus to him: "What misfortune hath befell thee? Why do I find thee so fallen away? Thy Flock is so too, it diminishes and grows worse and worse every day, and gives less Milk then ordinarily it used to do."

Thereupon the Shepherd told him the story of the young Lady. He was astonished at it, and said to him; "At what time does this Lady come thus to see thee?" "In the evening (reply'd the Shepherd) when the Sun is ready to set." Upon that *Gebirus* lighted off his Beast, and said to the Shepherd; "Take off thy Garment and strip thy self."

The Shepherd obey'd, and the King put on the Shepherds garment, cloathed himself like him, and sate in his place. A while after behold the young Lady, who was already come out of the Sea, comes to salute him. He returned the salute, and she said to him; "Wilt thou wrestle any more on the same terms we have done already?" "With all my heart," said the King.

Immediately she came near him, and endeavoured to cast him down; but *Gebirus* gave her a fall presently, and violently crush'd her. Whereupon she said to him, "You are not my ordinary match." "No," said the King. "Since I cannot avoid being taken (said she) put me into the hands of my former match; for he has treated me courteously, and I have tormented his heart many times: mean time he hath captivated me as I have captivated him. In requital I will teach you the way to complete this Building, as you desire."

After therefore he had put her into the hands of the Shepherd, he desired her to tell him whence came that which happened every day to his Building; and if there were any means to make it continue in that condition whereto they brought it.

"There are," reply'd she; "but know, great Prince, that the Land of *Egypt* is a Land of Enchanters, and that the Sea there is full of Spirits and Demons, which assist them to carry on their affairs, and that they are those who take away your Buildings." "But what means is there to prevent it?" said the King. "To do that (said she) you shall make great Vessels of Transparent glass, with Covers thereto, which may keep the waters from entering in; and you shall put into them Men well skill'd in Painting, and with them Meat and Drink for a week, and Cloaths, and Pencils, and whatever is necessary for Painting. Then you shall stop the Vessels well, after you have fastened them at the top with strong Cords, and ty'd them to the Ships, and then you shall let them go into the Sea like Anchors, and you shall put at the top of the cords little Bells, which the Painters shall ring; and then I will tell you what it is requisite that you should do."

Painters in the bottom of the Sea.

Gebirus did all she had ordered him; he caused the Vessels to be made, and brought the Painters before her, who heard all she said to him; then he promised them great wealth and honours, and they promised him to do his business. They therefore put these Vessels to the bottom of the Sea, after they had stopped them well above, and fastened them with cord, and left them there a week: after which the Painters rung the Bells, and presently they were taken out of the water, and they opened the Vessels, out of which they took along with them the Draughts they had made. The King presented them afterwards to the young Lady *Marina,* and she said to them; "Make now Statues of Copper, and Tin, and Stone, and Earth, and Wood, resembling your Draughts, and set them on the Sea-side, before the Buildings you shall make: for then the Beasts of the Sea, when they shall come out to demolish your Buildings as they are wont, seeing those Figures, will imagine that they are companies of Demons like themselves, come to fight with them, and they will presently return to the place whence they came."

The Painters and Gravers did so, and by that means *Gebirus* completed his Structure as he desired. After that he spoke thus to the Nymph, "Behold all the Money we had hath been expended in the Building of this City; know you not where there is some Treasure in this Land? for the City is not yet finished, and we have no more Money." "There is (reply'd the Nymph) in this ruin'd City (she meant *Alexandria)* on the one side of your Building an empty round place, and about that place there are seven Pillars, **The seven Tombs.** with a brazen Statue standing on the top of each of them; Sacrifice to every one of those Statues a fat Bull, and cause the Pillar under it to be rubb'd with the blood of the Bull, then perfume it with the hair of his Tail, and with somewhat you shall cause to be shaved from his Horns and his Hoofs, and speak thus to it: 'Behold the Offering I make to thee, let me therefore have what is about thee.' Having done and said this, measure from every Pillar, on that side that the Statue upon it shall have its face turned, the space of a hundred Cubits, then cause people to dig there. You shall do all this when the Moon is at full, and *Saturn* direct. After you have digg'd fifty Cubits, you will find a great Floor; cause it to be rubb'd with the gall of the Bull, then taken away; for thence you will descend into a Cave 50 Cubits in length, at the end whereof you will find a Store-house made of stone, and made fast with a Lock, the Key whereof shall be under the Threshold of the Door; take it and rub the Door with what shall be left of the Bulls gall, and perfume it with the shavings of the Horns and Hoofs of the same Animal, and the hair of his Tail; for then it shall open. You shall afterwards expect till the Winds that shall be within get out; when they shall be calmed, enter; for you will meet with an Idol of Brass, having about its neck a plate of the same metal, on which you will find written whatever is in the Store-houses, of Silver, precious Stones, Statues, and other Wonders. Take thereof what you please, but make no stay before a dead person whom you shall find there, and let not what there is upon him of Jewels and precious Stones give you occasion of envy. Do afterwards as much to every Pillar and its Statue, you will find there again as much Wealth in a like Store-house; for they are the Tombs of seven Kings buried with their Treasures."

Gebirus having heard this discourse of the Nymph was extremely satisfy'd. He punctually did all she had said to him, and found great wealth, which cannot be described, and abundance of rare and admirable things. By this means he completed the Building of the City, which coming to the knowledge of *Charoba,* she was very much displeased thereat, and fell into a great disturbance. For her intention was only to weary out the King, and to reduce him to an impossibility. They say that among other Miracles which *Gebirus* found there, there was a little golden Cabinet, seal'd up with an unknown Seal; and that having open'd it, he found in it a Box made of red precious Stones, and full of a green Powder, in the form of a *Collyrium,* (or Eye-Medicine) the mouth of which Box was in like manner stopped with a green Emerald, and that upon the Cabinet there was written; *"He who shall use this Collyry shall grow young again, his hair shall grow black again, and his sight shall be clear'd, that he shall be able to see all sorts of Spirits."* He there found also the Figure of an *Icneumon* (or *Egyptian* Rat) made of Gold, which being exposed to the Air the Sky was overcast, and immediately there came Rain. He there found moreover a Seat of Marble, on which there was the Figure of a Raven, made of a black Stone, which being questioned spoke, and answered to what was asked of it. They say that in each of those Store-houses there were ten Miraculous things, which it would be long to declare one after another;

wherefore we shall content our selves with what we have briefly said thereof. After *Gebirus* (saith the Author) had acquitted himself of the Building of the City, he sent the tidings of it to *Charoba,* and invited her

Charoba's Nurse defeats *Gebirus* and his Army.

to come and see it. It was her Nurse who brought her the news, and withall said to her, "Fear not, nor give your self any trouble concerning him." Then presently she carried to *Gebirus* a piece of Tapistry of great value, and said to him; "Put this on the Seat in which you shall sit, and afterwards divide your people into three parties, and send them to me that I may give them a Treatment such as they deserve. When the first party shall be about a third part of the way, you shall send away the second, then afterwards the third, to the end they may be near us dispersed in the Countrey for our safety."

He did so, and in the mean time she continued sending to him precious Houshold-stuff, till such time as she knew that they were upon their way, and that he had sent to her the third part of his Army. Then she caused to be set for them Tables, replenish'd with Poisoned Meats and Drinks, and when they were come to the Tables, her Servants Men and Maids made them stay and sit down to eat, standing all about them with Umbrellos or Fans; so that they all died from the first to the last. They afterwards quitted that Post, and passed to the other, where the second party met them, whom they treated after the same manner. Then they removed to the third, and serv'd them as they had done the others, so that all died. After that she sent word to the King, that she had left his Army in her own City, and in her Castle and thereabouts, for the safety of her Women; and that she would be served by his Attendants, who should be about him ready to obey him. Accordingly she went to his Palace, accompanied by her Nurse and some of her meaner Women, who were with her, and carried Perfumes in Porcelain Dishes. He rose up and went to meet her, and immediately her Nurse put about him a sumptuous Robe, but poisoned, which she had prepared for that purpose; and blew a Fume into his face, which in a manner deprived him of his senses; then she sprinkled him with a water which she had, which loosened all his members, and dislocated all his joynts so that he fell to the ground in a swound. Then she opened his veins, and emptied them of all his bloud, saying, "The bloud of Kings is an excellent remedy." Her Nurse came up to him, and said to him; "Is the King well to night?" "Mischief on your coming hither, (replied he;) may you be treated accordingly." "Do you stand in need of any thing (replied she) before you taste death?" "I do," said he; "I would intreat thee to cause these words to be engraved upon one of the pillars of the Castle: '*I Gebirus the son of Gevirus the Mutaphequian, who have caused Marble to be polished, and the hard red stone and the green to be wrought; who have been possessed of Gold and Precious stones; who have built Palaces, and raised Armies; who have cut through Mountains, who have stopped Rivers with my arm: with all this my power, and my might, and my prowess, and my valour, I have been circumvented by the artifices of a Woman, weak, impotent, and of no worth; who hath deprived me of my understanding, and taken my life, and discomfited my Armies. Whoever therefore is desirous to prosper, though there be no prosperity in this world, let him have a care of the wilely subtilties of Women. This is the advice I give those who shall come after me. I have no more to say.*'"

Charoba thereupon commanded his head to be cut off, and that it should be set upon the gate of the City of *Memphis;* which was put in executtion by her people. After that she caused the Tower of *Alexandria* to be built, and to be graved thereon her own name, and that of *Gebirus,* and what she had done to him, and the time when the City had been built. Her fame came to the ears of Kings, who respected and esteemed her, and made submissions and proffers of obedience to her. She did since that many miraculous things in *Egypt:* among others she caused Castles and Bridges to be made upon the Frontiers, and put Garrisons of Souldiers therein, to be a Guard, and to repell Enemies on which side soever they came to plunder them. They say that *Gebirus* made this discourse to her at the point of death; "O *Charoba,* triumph not at my death, for there will happen to thee a day like this, and yet much longer: such is the custom of Fortune."

She troubled not her self at what he said, but she had not lived above a year after him, when having imbarqu'd upon the *Nile* in a small Vessel which she had, to take the air by Moon-light, on one side of the Pyramids; and being afterwards gone ashore to ease nature, attended by her Men and Women-servants who were about her: whilest she was in the height of her mirth and jollity she trod on a Serpent, which stung her in the heel, and made her immediately lose her sight. "Wo is me!" cried she. "It will prove nothing (Madam)" replied her Attendants. "You are deceived," said she; "the day which *Gebirus* threatened me withall is come."

Charoba's death.

Accordingly she died he next morning.

The *Egyptians* made King in her stead her Cousin-german *Dalic;* or rather (as others affirm) they made Queen her Cousin *Dalica:* for she had continued a Virgin, and was never married. *Dalica* was endowed with a great understanding, prudence, and conduct; and wanted not beauty. She caused the body of *Charoba* to be embalmed in *Camphire,* and brought into the City which she had built on the West side. For *Charoba* had caused to be prepared for her there a Tomb, embellished with all sorts of ornaments; and had appointed for Inhabitants of the City a great number of Priests, and Artizans, and Doctors, and Military persons. That City continued in a flourishing condition and populous, till it was ruined by *Nabuchodonosor* upon the Conquest of *Egypt. Dalica* reigned 70 years, and then died. King *Ablin* reigned after her, and after him the *Valide,* son of *Domegus* the *Amalekite;* and after him his son the *Rajan,* son of the *Valide,* who was the *Pharao* of *Joseph;* and after him his son *Magadan,* and after him his son *Axames,* and after him his son *Lates,* and after him *Tolma* the *Coptite,* otherwise called the *Valide,* son of *Masgab,* who was the *Pharao* of *Moses,* and who governed unjustly and tyrannically, attributing to himself what belonged not to him; wherefore *Moses* destroyed him, after he had given him the space of 400 years to be

Dalica Queen of *Egypt.*

Kings of *Egypt* after her.

converted, and drowned him and all his people, and all the *Egyptians* who had followed him, in the Red Sea, by the virtue of his Rod, according to the Decree of the Malediction of God, as we shall relate hereafter if God give us leave. Some would have the *Pharao* of *Joseph* to be the same with that of *Moses,* grounding their conjecture on what Almighty God said of him; "*A Believer of the house of Pharao said thus, Joseph is already come to you heretofore;*" and the rest of the verse. God knows how it is.

AN ABRIDGMENT OF
The Second Part of the Book
OF THE *PRODIGIES OF EGYPT.*

The Reverend Prelate the Doctor *Murtadi,* the Son of *Gaphiphus,* the Son of *Chatem,* the Son of *Molsem,* the *Macdesian;* the *Sapheguian,* Gods mercy upon him, saith, (citing his Author) That the Apostle of God (Gods peace and mercy be with him) said what follows: "When I was raised to Heaven I saw two Rivers, and I asked *Gabriel* which they were. He answered me thus; 'They are the *Nile* and *Euphrates.*'"

Words of *Mahumet* advantageous to *Egypt.*

The Son of *Guebasus* says, that the same Apostle of God (Gods peace and mercy be with him) spoke thus: "The All-mighty and All-good God hath caused to descend from Paradise upon the earth five Rivers; *Sichone,* which is the River of the *Indies; Gichone,* which is the River of *Balca;* the *Tigris* and *Euphrates,* which are the two Rivers of *Gueraca;* and the *Nile,* which is the River of *Egypt.* He made them descend from one of the Springs of Paradise, seated at the lowest of its stories upon the wings of *Gabriel,* (Gods peace be with him) and hath committed them to the custody of the Mountains, causing them to flow upon the earth, and making them useful for men, for divers conveniencies of their Lives."

And that is it which the Almighty saith; *"And we have made the Waters of Heaven to descend after a certain measure, and have appointed them their habitation upon earth; and we;"* and the rest of the verse. When the time of the going forth of *Gog* and *Magog* was come, Almighty God sent *Gabriel*, (Gods peace be with him) who took up by his Order from above the earth the *Alcoran*, and *Science*, and the *Black Stone*, and the *Support*, which is the place of *Abraham*, (Gods peace and mercy be with him) and the Shrine of *Moses*, (Gods peace be with him) with what was within it, and these five Rivers mentioned before. All this was taken up into Heaven. And that is it which the Almighty saith, *"And it is in our power to carry it away: and when I have taken up these things from the earth, the Inhabitants of it were the choice part of Religion and of the World."* And citing his Authors he speaks thus: "I have heard *Abulamamus* the *Bahelian*, and *Gabdollus* the son of *Basar* the *Mazenian*, who said; The Apostle of God (Gods peace and mercy be with him) one day called his Companions together, and said to them; The All-mighty and All-good God shall enable you to conquer *Egypt* after me. Make your advantage of the Fruits it brings forth: for he who wants money wants not honesty for that. *Egypt* is the Mother-nurse; it supplies wherewithall to live plentifully. Other Countries want her, but she does not stand in need of any other Countrey." He said to them also; "I have received it from *Gabriel*, that God hath sent four Rivers out of Paradise; the first of Wine, the second of Milk, the third of Water, and the fourth of Honey."

Then the All-mighty and All-good God said; *I have made my particular standard of the Lord of Rivers,* which is the *Nile,* in the book of God, and it is a River flowing out of Paradise.

Megavius ask'd *Cabay* and said to him, "I ask thee in the Name of the great God, giver of all good things, Doest thou find in the Book of the All-mighty and All-good God, that God declares his Will to this *Nile* twice a year?" "I do," replied he: "God tells her when he would have her flow, and saith to her, 'The All-mighty and All-good

Augmentation of the *Nile*.

God commands thee to flow,' and she flows as far as God orders her: and after that God discovers his Will to her, and saith to her, 'O

Nile, the All-mighty and All-good God commands thee to return to thy former condition, and to praise him.'"

Jezidus the son of Chebibus speaks thus of it; "When Moses called upon God against Pharao and his Servants, God hindered the Nile to encrease as much as it would have done. Then they had recourse to Moses, and desired him to pray to God for them, which he did, hoping they would believe in God. This happened during the time they adored the Cross. The next morning God had augmented the Nile for them 16 full Cubits."

Quisus the son of Chagegus affirms, that somebody related it to him, that Gamrou the son of Gazus, after he had conquered Egypt, having entered into it in the moneth of Baune, which is one of the barbarous moneths, the Inhabitants of the Countrey came to him and said, "Lord Commander, our Nile which you here see governs its course according to a Law which it inviolably observes." "What Law is that?" says Gamrou. "When the 12th. of this present moneth is come (said they) we take a young Maid, a Virgin, from her Father and Mother, after we have satisfied them both, and made them condescend to what we would do according to the custom, we dress and adorn her with Jewels and Sumptuous Clothes, then we bring her in the night time, and cast her into the Nile, and immediately it increases, and spreads, and raises its course." "This cannot be continued (said Gamrou) according to the Mussulman Law; for the Mussulman Law destroyes the profane customs that have been in vogue before her."

A Virgin Sacrific'd to that end.

So the Moneth Banne, and the Moneth Abibe, and the Moneth Mesri, pass'd away, and the Nile encreased not its course, neither more nor less, so that the Inhabitants of Egypt were upon thoughts of leaving the Countrey. Gamrou seeing that, writ of it to the Commander of the Faithful Omar, (Gods peace be with him) acquainted him with what the Egyptians had said to him, and desired to know his resolution thereupon. Omar made him answer in these terms: "*After that, O* Gamrou, *you have done what you ought to have done upon that occasion, for the* Mussulman *Law abolishes the evil customs that have preceded it. But I have inclosed a Note within the fold of this present Letter, when you have read it, take that Note and cast it into the* Nile, *and God will do what he shall think fit."* Gamrou having receiv'd the Letter, took the Note out of it, on which he found these words written: *"In the Name of God, Gracious and Merciful; God bless* Mahumet *and his Family; From* Gabdol Omar, *the son of* Chettabus, *Commander of the* Faithful, *to the* Nile *of* Egypt." *After that, "If thou hast flow'd hitherto onely by thy own virtue, flow no more; but if it hath been the Only and Almighty God that hath caused thee to flow, we pray the Only Great and All-mighty God to make thee flow again. Gods peace and mercy be with* Mahumet *the Unlettered Prophet, and his Family."* Gamrou took the Note, and came to the *Nile* one day before they celebrated the Feast of the *Cross,* the *Egyptians* and others being ready to leave the Countrey; for they could not carry on their affairs, nor subsist therein, but by the annual overflowing of the *Nile:* but the next morning they found that God had caused the Waters to rise sixteen Cubits in one night. So God delivered the *Mussulmans* out of that affliction; praise and thanksgiving be to him for it.

Gabdol the son of *Gamrou,* the son of *Gasus,* (Gods peace be with them both) speaks thus of the *Nile;* "The *Nile* of *Egypt* is the Lord of Rivers; God obliges all the Rivers from the the East to the West to wait on it at the time of its overflowing; he turns them all into its Chanel, and increases its course with their waters. When God would have the *Nile* of *Egypt* to overflow, for the convenience of the Inhabitants, the other Rivers lend it their waters, and God causes new Springs to rise out of the Earth. When its course is risen to the height that God would, he orders the waters to return to their Sources. God All-mighty speaks thus of it; *'And we have made them to issue out of the Gardens and the Fountains, and out of the manured lands, and out of the precious places.'*

"The Gardens (saith he) were the two sides of the *Nile,* from its beginning to its end, upon both the Banks, between *Syene* and *Rasid. Egypt* had then sixteen Cubits of water, accounting from the lowest part of the flat Countrey. They empty'd and filled the Chanels and Rivulets of it every year. What was yet more noble were the Places appointed for Orations, which were a thousand in number, upon which they called upon God for *Pharao,* and they pray'd him to grant him a long life, and to make him liberal, and of easie access."

Aburaham the *Semaguian,* in his Comment upon these words of *Pharao,* "Is not the Kingdom of Egypt mine?" and the rest of the Verse, speaks thus: "There was then no greater King upon Earth then the King of *Egypt;* for all the other Kings stood in need of *Egypt.* All the Currents were made with the hands of Men, and the Aqueducts, and the Fountains, and the Bridges, all according to Measure and Geometrical proportion. They drew them out of the *Nile,* and brought them into all their Houses, and into all their Castles, and made them flow under the places of their Habitations, detaining them when they pleased, and dismissing them in like manner." *Mechacol,* the Son of *Tabicus,* speaks of it in these terms; "I have read a hundred Books upon the Law of *Moses,* and have found in one of them, that there are seven Climats in the world, which pray to God every year weeping and crying, and say; O Lord, send plenty into *Egypt,* and make its *Nile* flow. For when *Egypt* is water'd we have Meat and Drink enough. Withall there is on our surface of Wild Beasts, and Reptiles, and Tame and Rational Creatures." *Gabdol* the son of *Gamrou* said; "By the true God, I know not any year, wherein the Inhabitants of *Egypt* went out of their Countrey, to seek a subsistence elsewhere. 'We shall never go out of it,' says one of them, 'if some enemy do not force us thereto.' Not so (reply'd he) but your *Nile* shall be swallowed under ground, so that there shall not be a drop of it left. It shall be full of Sand-banks, and the wild Beasts of the Earth shall devour its Fishes."

Pharao.

Jezidus the son of *Chebibus* speaks thus of it; "The *Nile* of *Egypt* in the time of *Pharao* and the Precedent Kings had People appointed to make its Chanels, to repair its Bridges and Banks, and to clear its Rivulets and Trenches of Oziers, Ordures, Paper-plants, and what ever might obstruct the course of the Water, when there was occasion, to the number of six score thousand Work-men, always ready to work Winter and Summer, receiving their pay Monethly out of the publick Treasury, as the Soldiery, as well by Sea as Land, receiv'd theirs out of the Kings Money." The son of *Lahigus* saith, that he heard it of one of *Alexandria,* that the *Nile* one day discover'd a Rock, on which there was somewhat written in the Roman Language, which was read, and signify'd as followeth: *"I do what is good, and he seems to forget it, but when I do what is evil, he remembers it well. He who is such will not be long ere he meet with a long repose."*

An Abridgement of what is said of *Pharao,* and how God destroy'd him by the Decree of his Divine Will. *Gali* the son of *Abutalchus* speaks thus of him. "*Pharao* King of *Egpyt* was a Dwarf, or little Man, but seven spans in height. Others say he was three Cubits high, and that his Beard was two Cubits long, so that when he sate, he drew one Cubit of it on the ground before him. He twisted up his Mustachoes, and put them above his two ears. When the water of the *Nile* was turned into Blood in the time of *Moses, Pharao* drunk the juice of Orange-leaves, with fine Sugar put into it. Some affirm he was of low Stature, mark'd with white spots, and that he trod on his Beard, it was so long." *Abubeker* the Truth-teller (Gods peace be with him) said that *Pharao* had lost all his Teeth. Others affirm he was of the Race of the *Amalekites*. Others say he had a large fleshy face. Others say they call'd him *Abumarus,* that is, *Married.* Others say he was a Weaver of *Ciprus,* an Inhabitant of *Ispahan,* and that *Haman* was his Associate; that both of them became poor, and lost all they had, so that necessity having forc'd them to quit the Countrey and run away, they came together into *Egypt,* and prevail'd so much by their sleights and artifices, that they became Masters of it, and that there happened to them what God revealed to *Mahumet,* (Gods peace and mercy be with him) as it is related by the son of *Gubasus*. Others say that *Pharao* was a *Coptite,* of a City named *Damra,* the most Western of any in *Egypt,* and that his name was *Dolmes*.

Mahumet the son of *Gali,* the son of *Gabdol* the *Teminian,* says thus: "A Barbarian *Egyptian* of the Inhabitants of *Copta,* skill'd, in the History of *Egypt,* and what concerns the nature and properties of the Countrey, told me that he found it written in one of their ancient

Sources of the *Nile*.

Books, that the *Nile* of *Egypt* hath its rising out of a Lake in the most remote Countries of the West, on both sides whereof the Kings of the Moores have their Habitarions; and that by the Lake there is a great Mountain, always covered with Snow Winter and Summer, out of which there falls down Water, besides many Springs that are in the Lake, and which do also supply some; and that it is thence the water of the *Nile* comes; which is afterwards augmented by Rains, which augmentation happens, in regard the Rains fall in Summer in the Countrey of the *Moors,* whence it comes that the *Nile* overflowes in Summer, and not in Winter in *Egypt;* that in all the former Climat, and in part of the Second, the rains fall in the Summer, and in like manner in *India,* and in *Sinda,* and in the other Countries, which are in the same latitude, as well in the East, as in the West."

Causes of its overflowing.

Jezidus the son of *Chebibus* saith, that *Moses* the son of *Nasirus* speaks thus: "O *Egyptians,* you know not what I would say, neither you nor any other Inhabitanr of *Egypt.* I have heard that one day the *Nile* became very low, in the time of *Pharao,* which oblig'd the Inhabitants of his Kingdom to come to him and say; 'Cause the *Nile* to flow according to its ordinary course, for behold our Cattel die, and such as are big bring forth before their time.' 'I am too much incens'd against you (replied *Pharao*) to be so easily appeas'd, and to restore you so soon the course of the *Nile.*' They departed, and after a moneth returned to him again, and said; 'The Cattel perish, the Trees dry up, all is spoiled and destroy'd: cause the *Nile* to flow for us.' 'I am not yet reconciled with you,' said he. 'If you make not the *Nile* flow as it is wont (replied they) we will make another God besides you.' This reply troubled him, but it was not in his power to do what they desired.

"His Visier *Haman* was he who knew his secrets, who disposed of all his affairs, who heard his complaints and eased him of his grief. He had slights and subtile insinuations, which neither *Pharao* nor any other man could imitate. One day *Pharao* spoke to him, onely they two together, and acquainted him with the discourse had passed between him and the *Egyp-*

tians, confessing to him that he could not do what they desired, and that that business of the *Nile* was beyond his strength. 'I cannot (said he) take any course in this case, nor find any means to satisfie them.mWhat do you advise me therein?' 'Is that all that troubles you?' says *Haman.* 'And what would you have me do in it?' replied the King. 'Great King (replied *Haman)* they have not bethought themselves of asking you a thing, which would have been much more impossible then this, and might have given them greater occasion to proclame your weakness in all places.' 'What is that?' replied the King. 'If any one of them (said *Haman)* had bethought him of requiring you to raise up his father or brother after their death, that would have been more difficult to you then the affair of the *Nile.*' 'Speak not of such things,' says *Pharao;* 'for Walls have ears. But what advice do you give me in the affair of the *Nile*?' 'Light off your Mule,' said *Haman;* 'and restore to every one what belongs to him, and the *Nile* will resume its course.' 'You know (replied the King) that hitherto I have not wronged any one, nor deprived my Subjects of any thing belonged to them, that I should restore it again: and as for my white Mule, I promise you never to get on her back any more.'

"He had a white Mule, which in swiftness no other Beast in *Egypt* could go before, or indeed come near. 'The Mule I mean (said *Haman)* is not the *animal* so called, but Arrogance and Pride. Humble your self before the God of *Moses* and *Aaron,* acknowledge in your self what you ought; give him thanks for his favours, and confess his Omnipotence and Unity: for you know well that he is the Creator and Preserver, and that you are one of his Servants, who can neither do him harm nor service. Pray him that he would cause the *Nile* to flow for his Servants, for he is merciful and meek; he is not hasty, and fears not that he hath not done a thing soon enough.' 'I will do it with all my heart,' said the King. 'You have at last found out a way to deliver me out of my trouble. Make an end (O *Haman)* as you have begun.' 'I shall not fail, said *Haman.*'

"The *Egyptians* came afterwards to him the third time, and said the same thing they had said to him the two former times. His answer was this: 'Repent you that you have disobeyed me.' 'We do repent us of it,' replied they. 'Go your ways (said the King) to the end of the Upper *Egypt,* clad and dressed the best you can.'

"They did so, and there remained in *Egypt* but such as were not able to go out of it. *Pharao* went up to them on his Mule; then he turned a little aside from them, alighted off his Mule, prostrated himself on the ground, and made his prayers to God in these terms: 'Great God, you know that I acknowledge there is none but you alone who can re-establish this *Nile* in its course, and that I am obliged to this people in a thing which is not within the compass of my power, and that I cannot keep my promise with them. Cause it therefore to flow for them as it was wont, and make me not infamous among them: for you are full of leity and goodness; you are not hasty, nor impatient, and fear not that you have not done a thing soon enough.'

"Immediately the *Nile* (saith he) swelled, and flowed after a more excellent manner then it had ever done before, or hath done since. Then *Pharao* came up to them and said; 'Return to your homes, for I have restored the *Nile* for you into its course.' They thereupon prostrated themselves all before him, and adored him, and then returned to their habitations, speaking continually of their King, and incessantly resounding his praises. He returned himself to his Castle, but *Gabriel* went to meet him by the way in the shape of a Shepherd, laid hold on the Bridle of his Mule, and said to him; 'Great King, do me justice against my Servant.' 'What has thy Servant done to thee?' said *Pharao.* 'I have a Servant (replied *Gabriel)* to whom I have been liberal of my kindnesses and favours, and yet he persecutes me, and those whom I love, and obliges those whom I hate: he is rebellious and disobedient to my commands, ungrateful, and not acknowledging the good I have done him, even so far as to say, he knows not who I am.' 'A very wicked Servant,' said *Pharao.* 'If you bring him to me, I will have him drown'd in the Red Sea, and shall not content my self for his punishment with the water of the *Nile,* which is sweet and pleasant.' 'Great King (replied *Gabriel)* let me have a Decree written to this purpose, that whereever I shall find him I may punish him according thereunto.'

"*Pharao* caused Paper and Ink to be brought, and caused to be written thereon the Condemnation of a Servant rebellious to his Master, who loves his enemies, and persecutes his friends; who disobeys and ill-treats him, who is ungrateful, and acknowledges not the kindnesses he hath received of him, making as if he knew him not, saying he knows not who he is; and order'd that he should be drown'd in the Red Sea.

"'Great King (said *Gabriel*) be pleased to sign this Decree.'

"*Pharao* sign'd, and seal'd it with his own Seal, and put it into his hands. *Gabriel* took it, and kept it as long as God commanded him. When the day of Submersion was come, *Pharao* being just upon the point of drowning, God having delivered *Moses* and his people from the waves, and having opened them a passage through the Sea, *Gabriel* came to *Pharao* with that Decree. 'What is this?' says *Pharao*. 'Open it (says *Gabriel*) and read what it contains.'

"*Pharao* opened it, and read it, and remembered it. 'You are (said *Gabriel* to him) the Servant whom this Decree mentions, and see here what you have decreed against your self. God is merciful and meek; he is not hasty, and is not afraid not to do a thing soon enough: Let him be praised and exalted, to the regret of those who attribute his Divinity to others.'"

Qualities of *Egypt*. As to the Qualities attributed to the Land of *Egypt* they say; It is the Relief of Men, and the Nursery of Nations: that those who live in it, love it; and that those who have left it, are troubled, and bemoan themselves to return into it: that its Inhabitants are subtile, and intelligent, and crafty, and deceitful; that they lie to such as live at a great distance from them, persecute such as are near, and are envious at the prosperity of others. Some one of them in one of the ancient Books saith, that in *Egypt* is the streight of Mountains, and the Separation described, and the reiterated Sea, and accustomed good: that it is the place of the destruction of the White and Flaxen-hair'd people, when they shall commit great devastations, and set up the Crosses, and make war against the Merciful, and persecute the Observers of the *Alcoran,* and the Nation of the Children of Mercy, when they shall come against it in the last times; and that every one of them shall receive the reward of his actions, and not one of them return into his Countrey.

The History of the *Egyptian* Slave.

One of the Ancients of *Egypt* made me a relation of his father, (God shew him mercy;) that in a Voyage he had made he had been taken by *French* Pirats in one of the Islands of the Sea, and sold by them to an Armourer, who made Arms for the King of that Island, with whom he had no rest night nor day, being continually imployed in blowing, beating on the Anvil, and carrying things of Iron, wherewith his Master loaded him beyond his strength. He continued there a long time, so that he became old and weak.

"Then (said he) as I slept one night, wearied with hard working, and overwhelmed with grief, after I had said the last prayer appointed for the evening, and implored the assistance of God, and put all the hope of my deliverance in him, I dreamt that I saw a man coming to me, who said, 'Friend, rejoyce at the good news I bring thee: thou shalt ere long be delivered out of thy afflictions. Be not troubled at the hardship thou art in, and the work thou doest: for the Arms thou makest, and those who shall bear them shall with Gods help be the prey of thy Brethren the *Mussulmans*. The *Romans* have a design to engage in a war against the *Mussulman* Countries; they will carry thee along with them whither they go, and God will deliver thee out of their hands.' I awaked thereupon very joyful, and gave thanks to God with great confidence. The labour and affliction became more light and supportable to me then before; for I was satisfied it was a true Vision from God. The first night after, the same person who ha already called me presented himself again before me in my Dream, and said to me; 'Pray to God in these terms: "O Great God, who hast compassion on Sinners, and keepest those who have stumbled from falling quite down, be merciful to thy Servant, who hath highly offended thee, and to all the *Musslmans* in general. For All-mighty God will deliver thee and bring thee out of the trouble wherein thou art."' I immediately did so, (said he) and the next year being come, the *French* (God prevent their evil designs) prepared for the War against the *Mussulman* Countries, putting their Horses and Arms, and all their Baggage in great Vessels, and taking the Sea. They caused me also to Embarque among the other Captives, whom they took along with them for their service, and to execute their Commands. We were a Moneth at Sea, and made little Progress, the Wind being not favourable. That Moneth past, there came a Wind which pleased them, and by means whereof they thought to compleat their voyage; whereupon they weighed Anchor, and took their course towards the Coast of *Egypt*. We advanced with that wind seven Days and seven Nights, till they came in sight of the Land of *Egypt*. They were very jocund among themselves, exalting their Crosses, ringing their Bells, and setting their Gospel in sight. They thus pass'd away some part of the night well satisfy'd in a certain road of the Sea: But about Midnight God sent a violent wind upon them, with a black Dust, and Thunder and Lightning, the Air was darkned, and the Sky grew black, and the Sea was so rough that the Waves rose up like high Mountains. Finding themselves ready to perish, and to see their Vessels split to pieces, they resolved to get out of that Road, fearing their Ships should fall foul one upon another in the Sea, and saying; 'Let us rather make for any Coast whereto the Sea shall cast us, though it were into the most remote parts of the world, and let us not stay here.' They therefore weighed Anchor, and hoised the Sails, and began to go as the wind drove them; so that there remained not one with another. The Ship wherein I was was forced by the wind upon the coast of *Alexandria,* so that we ran aground on the right side of the City near the *Phaos*. Immediately the *Mussulman* vessels came to us, and seized our Ship and all that was in it, and made a great booty of Gold and Silver, Arms and Baggage. For my part I was delivered by the mercy of God, with five other Slaves who were with me in the Ship. I returned to my Countrey, and related my dream to the *Mussulmans,* who rejoyced thereat, and thanked God for the kindness he had shewn me: May he be praised for ever, at the beginning and at the end of all things; he who is the first and the last."

This is one of the most miraculous kindnesses and favours which God hath done to the Inhabitants of *Egypt,* which God preserve.

Some make another Description of *Egypt*, saying that it is a Land wherein there are for famous places *Qirata*, and *Ecbata*, and *Damiette*, and *Igora*, and *Rebata*,

Other qualities of *Egypt*.

whose River is clear, and its waters sweet, where diseases are dispell'd, and hope crown'd with effect; where the vicissitude of things passes without confusion, and without disturbance. Those who come thither with an intention to do ill, return thence without accomplishing their design; those who contrive the destruction of it, meet with their own; those who have their Habitations therein are in safety, and make their advantage; and those who leave it, repent them of it. It was said one day to an excellent person, "What say you of *Egypt?*" "What (reply'd he) would you have me say of that Province? Those who leave it repent them that they ever did it. It quels Kings and destroys them, and supports the poor. All those who have an affection for it, find there how to employ themselves about what they like best, according to their power."

An Extract of the Annals of the *Geranian*: "An ancient *Egyptian* of the chiefest of the Countrey relates, as having taken it out of *Abuquilus* the *Mogapherian*, the Pacifier, whom *Gabdol* the Son of *Nasilus* had taught; That *Noah* (Gods peace and mercy be with him) after he had divided the Earth among his Children, had a numerous Posterity, by whom he caused it to be Inhabited and Cultivated. The Kingdom of *Egypt* fell to *Masar*, the son of *Bansar*, the son of *Cham*, the son of *Noah*, who had many children, and by them a great progeny. *Noah* had prayed God for *Masar*, or *Mesraim*, that he would give him his benediction in his Land, and to his Children after him; whence it came that the Land was fertile and abundant to them; its *Nile* overflow'd, all its quarters fructify'd, its Cattel were multiply'd, its Mines had been discovered. The Trees bore Dates as big as Pillars: The Grains of Wheat were as big as Hens Eggs, soft as Butter, and sweet as Hony. There were some among them who particularly apply'd themselves to the Mines of Topazes, which are adjoyning to the Countries of *Syene*, at the upper part of High *Egypt*, opposite to the Provinces of the *Nubians*, whom *Mesrai* the son of *Bansar* had appointed for his Lieutenants upon the Frontiers of of *Egypt,* saying unto them; 'Be my Lieutenants over the Frontiers of this Land,' whence they were called *Nubians,* that is to say *Lieutenants.* One man took out of the Mines such a piece of Tapaze as that he might make a Table of it, with Dishes and Trenchers to set upon it. All their Vessels were Marble, and Gold, and Silver, and Topaze. The *Nile* cast on its Shores certain Leaves which came from Paradise, so Odoriferous that they needed not other perfumes. There were on both sides of the *Nile* Gardens, from *Syene* quite to the extremities of the Land of *Egypt,* so that a man walking along the Banks of the *Nile* had a perpetual coolness and shade, and had not his head any way incommodated by the heat of the Sun. The first City which *Mesraim* founded in the Land of *Egypt* was *Memphis.* There was not then in *Egypt* any thing that incommodated the Inhabitants of the kind of Serpents, or other venemous Beasts. They lived along time without being impaired by old age, sickness, or infirmity, and without having any having any hatred or envy one against another, till they alter'd the Religion of their Ancestor *Noah,* (Gods peace and mercy be with him) and changed his Law. Then the Devil (Gods enemy) got dominion over them by his craft and circumventions, distracted their affairs, and sowed discord and enmity amongst them. He made them delight in the worship of Idols, so that they adored them during the space of five hundred years; whence it came that their fruits diminish'd, their Cattel perished, and their Mines became barren. There came out against them mischievous Creatures out of the Earth, and out of the Sea; the shade forsook them, the Benedictions were taken away from them, and exemplary punishments fell upon them. *'Certainly God changes not the state of a Nation, untill it be changed of it self;'* and the rest of the Verse. Thus their affairs went worse and worse, till the King of the *Amalekites* came out of *Syria* to War against them.

"The King of *Egypt* then was *Cophtarim,* the son of *Cophtim,* the son of *Masar,* the son of *Bansar.* The King of the *Amelekites* was named *Gainon,* from whom *Baitgainon* in the Land of *Syria* derives its name. He was insolent and impious, and very corpulent. He had to his Uncles among the *Amalekites Gebirus* the *Mutaphequian,* and his Brother *Gebrin.* This King then came with his Forces, consisting of a thousand *Amalekite* Lords, and six hundred thousand Soldiers. They entred into the Land of *Egypt,* and Encamped upon its Frontiers on the side of the great Banks. *Gainon* Warred against the Inhabitants of *Egypt* for the space of a Moneth; after which he defeated them, and took possession of the Countrey, *Cophtari* and his Forces having forsaken it, and got into the Desarts of the West. The *Amalekite* continued in *Egypt* without injuring any person; for he said to the the *Egyptians,* 'You are the Inhabitants of the Countrey, his Subjects who is possessed of it, and his Servants who is Conquerour.'

"He afterwards gave them security as to his part, and appointed over them for Governour his Brother named *Gamrou,* on whom he bestow'd for Visier a *Coptite* named *Zephton,* who was then of the principal Inhabitants of *Egypt,* being there possess'd of a great estate; and having many Friends and others inclin'd to his party. His skin was black, and he resembled the children of *Cham. Gamrou* founded a City upon the *Nile*'s side, which he named *Gamra;* and ordered his Visier *Zephton* to build such another opposite to it. The Visier obeyed him, and named the City he built *Zephta,* each of them deriving its name from the Founder. They caused them both to be built, and whitened with great care; and Vault to be made therein under ground, and Aqueducts coming out of the *Nile,* and compassing the publick places. They also caused Walls and Trenches to be made about their Cities, enrich'd them with Villages and Farms, ordering Justice and Equity to be strictly observ'd in the Land of *Egypt.* They took but the tenth part of the profits of the Dairies and Farms. In the mean time *Gainon* got Provisions together, and fitted his Army to pursue *Cophtarim* and his People, who were fled towards the West. They pursued them so closely, that they forced them to enter into *Afri,* and to take refuge on a Mountain called the Mount of *Sosa,* where *Cophtarim* and his People Fortify'd themselves. There was on the descent of the Mountain a Castle built by one of the Children of *Cham,* very high and inaccessible. They held out stifly in that Castle, and got into it their goods. There was on one side of the Castle a Spring of fresh water, which occasioned them to put their Cattel and Horses that way. *Gainon* the *Amalekite* came and Encamped about the Castle, and Besieged it. That Siege lasted two Years; for they play'd upon him with Stones and Arrows, and he could do them no hurt; whereupon he caused Trenches to be made about them, and pressed not upon them, having resolved to take them by a long Siege. He therefore caused Houses and Huts to be made in the Plain; his Visier *Gamrou* relieving him with Money and Provisions, which he sent out of *Egypt*. They grew at length so confident, that they began to neglect the business of *Cophtarim* and his People; so that at last in a Winter night, the weather being cold, they entered into their Tents, and fell a Drinking, having no Guard abroad, because they had no distrust. *Cophtarim* had Spies among them, who presently gave him notice of that opportunity, and told him the Enemies were all Drunk, and immoveable as dead men; and if he let pass that night without taking advantage of the posture they were in, he should never escape out of their hands. Upon this intelligence *Cophtarim* came out of the Castle, accompany'd by his Infantry onely without Horse. His People being set upon the enterprise, he divided them into four Battallions, and ordered them at the same time to set upon the four quarters of *Gainon*'s Camp. They gave a great shout, and fell a cutting them to pieces, not one of them making any resistance. The slaughter continued all night till the next morning: those who escaped fled, some one way, some another, not knowing which way to go, and afterwards dyed of hunger and thirst. *Cophtarim*'s men took all their Baggage, their Cattel, their Horses, and their Money, and took King *Gainon* Prisoner, with the chiefest Lords of his Court. King *Gainon* recovered not himself out of his Debauch till they had bound him with Chains of Iron weighing fifty pound. They set him on a Camel, and immediately took their way towards *Egypt*, joyful and well satisfy'd. This news coming to *Gamrou Gainon*'s Lieutenant, he secretly packed up for his departure out of *Egypt*, with those that were about him. His Visier *Zephton* followed him with his Baggage and Equipage, and his Family, and those of his party. They got both of them into *Syria*. *Cophtarim* and his Forces returned in good order, with Colours flying, marching night and day, not making any stop upon any occasion whatsoever, till he got into his Countrey, and had put on his

Arms, and was advantageously dressed, and his Soldiers in like manner; causing to march before him *Gainon* bound and chained, and the Camels loaden with the Heads of his Favourites who had been killed, and their Cattel, and their Horses. The *Egyptians* went to meet him, joyful and glad of his coming, after they had beautified and adorned the City for his reception. *Cophtarim* came and lodged in his Royal Palace with great joy, and caused it to be publickly Proclaim'd that his intention was to have Justice and Equity, and good manners to flourish. He ordered also that *Gamra* and *Zephta,* the Cities built by *Gamrou* and *Zephton,* should be demolished; as well out of the horrour he had for their Names, as to give a good presage of their punishment, saying, He would not leave in *Egypt* any track of the *Amalekites.* Wherefore the *Coptites* have it among their Proverbs, Gainon *was blind, and* Zephton *covered with Infamy.* When any one digs the ground, and finds it so hard that he cannot get forward, they say of him, *He hath met with* Zephton's *good Fortune.* Mean time, the chiefest among them put *Cophtarim*'s action among the Stratagem of the *Coptites,* inasmuch as his flight (say they) was a mischievous subtilty against *Gainon,* and not an effect of the fright he had put him into; for they will ever be sly and subtile. The tracks of the two Cities *Gamra* and *Zephta* continued a long time in the same condition: they were afterwards both rebuilt by one of the Kings, then destroy'd again by *Nabuchodonosor,* when he entered into *Egypt,* and wasted it. Then when those who were remaining of the Inhabitants of *Egypt* return'd thither with *Belsa* the son of the *Coptess,* when he entered into *Egypt* after his death, that is, after the death of his Father *Nabuchodonosor,* they advised him after he had build the Castle of *Cira,* and the Church of *Mugalleca,* and the others, to built also upon the ground of the City of *Gamrou,* and that which was opposite thereto upon the *Nile,* but he would not. Yet they say concerning these two Cities, that a long time after there were two Villages built upon their Ruines, which were called by their names, and that those names have continued to them. God knows how it is, how ere it be kept secret from men."

Gamra and *Zephta.*

Omar.   They relate that when the Commander of the Faithful, *Omar* the son of *Chettabus* (Gods peace be with him) came into *Syria,* to receive the Keys of *Jerusalem,* according to what *Abugabidas* had writen to him of it, in regard the Patricians of the *Romans,* who were then in *Syria,* had intreated him to do it: when he was come near them he made a halt at a Village not far from *Jerusalem,* and continu'd there some time, during which the Governour of the City sent a Spy to him, saying; "Go thy ways, and observe the King of the *Arabians,* who comes hither to take possession of our Lands, and the Patrimony of *Caesar,* and return quickly to tell me how he looks; and describe him so to me, that I may know him, as well as if I had seen him my self."

The Spy came away, and made a shift to get just over against *Omar,* and view'd him as he sate on a She-Camel he had, clad in a Wollen Garment, mended with a piece of Sheep-skin, made as it were into a thread on that side towards the Sun, which had already burnt and blacken'd his face, with a bag hanging behind him, into which having put his hand, he pulled out pretty big pieces of Barley-bread; and with his Fingers struck off the husks, saying, *"In the Name of God;"* then he did eat till he was satisfied, and afterwards took a Bottle of Leather, which he carry'd with him full of water, and quench'd his thirst, saying after that, *"Praise be to God."* The Spy brought this news to the Patrician who sent him, and describ'd in what posture he had seen him; whereupon the Patrician continued along time without saying any thing, and then he spoke thus to such as were about him:

"Grant these people all they desire, for otherwise there is no way to be rid of them without fighting with them, and they have the favour of Heaven. Their Law and their Prophet enjoins them Humility, and Modesty, and Compliance; and these qualities lead to advancement and dominion. This description proceeds from that little party which appears above all the Inhabitants of the Earth. Their Law shall abolish all the Laws. My Father predicted this to me, having learnt it of his Father, who had received it from his Grand-father. They shall take the Kingdom of *Egypt* by force. There shall be in that Province Mosqueys and Temples, wherein they shall make their Prayers, the noise whereof shall be heard, like the humming of Bees. Their Empire shall extend to the Eastern parts of the World, and to the Western, and even to the end of the World."

Afterwards the Patrician sent to *Omar* (Gods peace be with him) to get his Protection for himself, and those of his House, and to agree wth him upon such conditions as he should desire, and be satisfy'd withall.

The *Solphian* (God shew him mercy) citing for Author the *Chasan,* son of *Ismael* the *Sarrabian,* in the Book of the Histories of *Egypt,* which he hath composed, speaks in these terms; "I have heard that the Land of *Alphiom* and its appurtenances were heretofore governed by the Prophet of God *Joseph,* (Gods peace be with him) according to the Revelation which he had had of it, and the Command given him by All-mighty God, and divided into three hundred and sixty Towns or Villages, as many as there are days in the year, and that with a design, which he brought to effect. For when the *Nile* fail'd any year, and that God heard not the Prayers made for the augmentation of its course, every one of those Villages supply'd *Egypt* with a days sustenance. There is no Countrey in the World that has been reduced and cultivated by Divine Revelation but this. There is not upon Earth a less and yet a more fertile Province, nor one that abounds in all sorts of good things, or is better furnished with Rivers. For if we compare the Rivers of *Alphiom* with those of *Bosra* and *Damas,* we shall find the former have the advantage. Many persons excellent for their wit and knowledge would have given us the number of its Chanels, and its free and common places; but they could not number them. Others have not medled with the Chanels, and have only set down the common places of that Countrey, which are not in the possession of any person *Mussulman,* or *Alien,* and whereof the mighty and the weak make equal advantage, and they have found about seventy sorts. 'Tis related of the *Mamunus* (God shew him mercy) that when he came to *Egypt* he sent for several of the chiefest Inhabitants of the Countrey, and among others two Learned men, one sur-

The Land of *Alphiom.*

The *Mamunus.*

named *Abulseriphus,* and the other *Saguidus,* the son of *Gaphirus,* of whom he enquired concerning the advantages of *Egypt,* and what things made it recommendable. *Suguidus* the son of *Gaphirus* made him a large discourse, after which he said to *Abulseriphus;* 'Do you also tell us what you know of the excellencies of your Countrey.'

"*Abulseriphus* praised God, and gave him thanks, and prayed for the Prophet (Gods peace and mercy be with him,) after which, 'Lord Commander of the Faithful (said he) *Joseph* the teller of Truth, (Gods peace and mercy be with him) after God had put the affairs of this our Province into his hands, and given him a Supremacy in it, obliged the Inhabitants to serve him in the Western parts, in a Land now called *Alphiom,* where he caused three hundred and sixty great Farms to be cultivated, as many as there are days in the year; so that the Village of each Farm furnished the Inhabitants of *Egypt* with a days fustenance. *Joseph* did this by Revelation, which he had had from his Lord. Had he made as many on the East side, we should have had more then we needed, all the provisions which might have been brought from the Eastside. For we have one day in the West.' 'It may be my Lord (said the *Mamunus)* the Sun rises in the West.' 'Before that (said *Abulseriphas)* the *Barbarians* will come.' 'Who told you that?' said the *Mamunus.* 'I found it (said *Abulseriphus)* in the Book of the Prophet *Daniel,* Gods peace be with him.' 'Is it necessary (said the *Mamumus,* that the *Barbarians* come?' 'It is, (said *Abulseriphus;)* insomuch that they shall come to the Land, that is, to the Countrey of *Emesse,* and then there will be no other Sanctuary but *Jerusalem,* and they shall have no other sustenance but Lupins.'

"He afterwards entertained him with long Discourses, which to avoid tedeousness we shall abridge. Then he said to him; 'Lord Commander of the Faithful, if our Countrey had no other advantage then what God says of it in the History of his Prophet *Joseph* (Gods peace be with him) when he speaks thus to the King, "*Give me the oversight of the Store-houses of the Land,*" it were enough.'"

Hasam the son of *Isaac,* says that *Joseph* (Gods peace and mercy be with him) when he was Master of *Egypt,* and highly favoured by the *Ra-*

jan his *Pharao,* after he had passed a hundred years of age, was envyed by the Kings Favourites and the Grandees of his Court, by reason of the great power he

The *Rajan, Joseph's Pharao.*

had, and the Kings great affection towards him, and that they one day spoke thus to him; "Great King, *Joseph* is now grown very ancient, his knowledge is diminished, his beauty is decay'd, his Judgment is impaired, and his Wisdom is departed from him."

Pharao liked not their remonstrances, and was so far from approving their discourses, that he gave them harsh language, so that for a good while after they durst not say any thing to him concerning *Ioseph:* but two years after they renew'd their formes envious discourses, whereupon the King said to them; "Tell me wherein you would have me make a tryal of his abilities."

Alphiom was then called *Geouna,* that is to say, the *Fenne,* and served for a Common Sewer to the Upper *Egypt,* and a passage for the water. They therefore agreed together about what they should propose to the King for the tryal of *Joseph,* (Gods peace and mercy be with him) and spoke thus to *Pharao;* "Command *Ioseph* to turn the water of *Geouna,* and force it thence, that you may have a new Province, and a new revenue."

The King thereupon sent for *Joseph,* and said to him; "You know how dear such a Daughter of mine is to me, and you see it is time I should assign her some place where she may be Mistress, and whereof the Revenues may be sufficient to maintain her: and I do not find any Lands besides my own which I can give her, unless it be *Geouna:* For that Land is neither too near, nor at too great a distance, and there is no coming into it of any side, unless it be through desart and dangerous places: the case will be the same with her, none can come near her on any side, but through desart and dangerous places."

Another besides *Hasam* says, that *Alphiom* is in the midst of *Egypt,* as *Egypt* is in the midst of other Countries, in regard one cannot get into *Egypt* on any side, but through places that are desart and full of danger.

"That is true, great King" (said *Joseph*) according to *Hasam*: "when does it please you to have it so? for it will be with the assistance of Allmighty God. The sooner the better *Joseph,* said the King."

God inspired *Joseph* what he had to do, and ordered him to cause three Chanels to be made; one Chanel coming out of High *Egypt,* from such a place to such a place; an Eastern Chanel, from such a place to such a place; and a Western Chanel. *Joseph* got men together to carry on this work, and caused the Chanel of *Manhi* to be digg'd, from the Upper part of *Asmounine* to *Lahon,* which he caused also to be digged afterwards. Then he caused the Chanel of *Alphiom* to be digged, and the Eastern Chanel, with another Chanel near it, named *Benhamet,* from the Villages of *Alphiom,* which is the Western Chanel, and draws from the Desart of *Benhamet* towards the West. By this means there remained no water in *Geouna.* That done, he got Labourers to cut down all the Reeds and Tamarisk that was in it, and carry it away, and then the *Nile* began to flow into it, and *Geouna* became pure and clean ground. The water of the *Nile* rose, and entered at the beginning of the *Manhi,* and flowed therein till it came to *Lahon,* whence it turned towards *Alphiom,* and entered into its Chanel, so that it was watered thereby, and made a Champain Countrey overflown by the *Nile.* The King (the *Rajan*) came to see it, with the Favourites who had given him that advice. After they had considered it, they were all astonished at the Wisdom and extraordinary Invention of *Joseph,* and began to say; "We know not whether we should more admire to see *Geouna* cleared of the water, and rid of the Reeds, and Paperplants, and Tamarisks, and Willows, whereof it was ful, or to see it o'reflown by the *Nile* after the levelling of the ground." Then the King said to *Joseph,* "How long were you *Joseph* in reducing this Land to the condition I now see it in?" "Seventy days," said *Joseph. Pharao* turned to his Favourites, and said to them; "It is not likely any one could have done it in a thousand days."

This occasioned the calling of that Land *Alphiom,* that is to say, *A Thousand Days*; and that very year it was sowen, and ordered as the rest of *Egypt.*

Jesidus the son of *Chebibus* says, that God made *Joseph* (Gods peace be with him) Master of *Egypt* at 30 years of age; and that after he had governed til 40 years the *Egyptians* said among themselves, *Joseph* is old, and hath not now the prudence he had heretofore: and that thereupon they devested him of the power which they had given him over them, and said to him; "Make your choice of some barren and useless ground, which we may give you to cultivate and people; for by that means we shall make trial of your prudence and judgment: and then if we find in your management thereof any thing to persuade us that your Understanding is yet in a tendency to advancement, we will re-establish you in your government."

The Acts of *Joseph* in *Egypt*.

Joseph considered the desart places of the appurtenances of *Egypt*, and chose the place now called *Alphiom*, which was presently given him. He brought thither from the *Nile* the Chanel of the *Manhi*, so that he made the water of the *Nile* flow all over the Land of *Alphiom*, and finished all their digging work in a years time. We hear also that he did it by inspiration from his Lord, and that he imployed therein a great number of Workmen and Labourers. The *Egyptians* considered that work, and saw that in all *Egypt* there was not any like or equal to the dead Land which *Joseph* had raised up again: whence it was concluded, that there was not a more excellent judgment, nor safer advice, nor better conduct, then that of *Ioseph;* and they thought themselves obliged to commit the affairs of *Egypt* into his hands. He governed them 130 years, that is, to his death, (Gods peace and mercy be with him.) Others affirm that he died at 130 years of age: God knows better then we do how it is. Some relate, as having it from *Hasam* the son of *Isaac,* that *Joseph* after his his re-establishment in the government of *Egypt* was well beloved by the Kings Favourites, and that they made their excuses to him. After which he spoke thus to the *Rajan;* "You have not yet seen, neither you nor your Favourites, all my wisdom and conduct can perform." "And what can you do more?" replied they. "I will put into

A second story of *Alphiom*.

Alphiom (said he) a Family of every City in *Egypt,* that they may there build a village for themselves; so that there shall be in *Alphiom* as many villages as there shall be Cities in *Egypt.* When they have quite built their villages, I will bring into every village as much water as shall be requisite, proportionably to the Land I shall have assigned it, so as there shall be neither too much nor too little. I will also have an Aqueduct come to every village, for the time that water cannot come there but under ground; and I will make it more deep for those who are seated high, and less deep for such as shall be low, according to the times and hours of the day and night. I will do all this for them by measure, so that every one shall have neither more nor less than is requisite." *Pharao* answered him thereupon; "This is of the Kingdom of Heaven, *Joseph.*" "It is so," said *Joseph.*

After that (says the Author) *Joseph* began the execution of that enterprise, causing the villages to be built, and assigning every one its limits. The first village built in *Alphiom* was called *Betiana,* and there *Pharao*'s Daughter had her habitation. He afterwards caused the Chanels to be digged, and the Bridges to be built: and when he had done that, he began to allot the Proportions of Land and Water, and there began Geometry, which before that was unknown in the Land of *Egypt:* for they onely followed *Joseph* in that, and it was one of the things which had been taught him by his Lord. They say also he was the first who measured the *Nile* in *Egypt,* and who established the *Nilometer* in the City of *Memphis.* After him the ancient *Cagalouca,* who was Queen of *Egypt,* and built the Wall of the ancient City, caused a *Nilometer* to be made at *Alsena,* where the Cubits are small; and another at *Achemima*: *Gabdolgueziz* the son of *Merouanes* caused also one to be made at *Choluan* in High *Egypt. Zaid* the son of *Asam,* during the *Caliphat* of the *Valide,* the son of *Gabdolmelic,* under the Reign of the House of *Ommie,* caused a *Nilometer* to be made in the Island which is opposite to *Masre,* between its Rivers; and this is greater then the others. As to that which is now used, it was built by the *Mamunus,* the son of *Harounes* the Law-observer; Almighty

The **Nilometer.**

God shew mercy to both: For when he entered into the Land of *Egypt*, he found the Christians negligent in measuring the water, when by the permission of God it encreased; which obliged him to speak thus; "This is a miracle of God, wherein he hath put a mystery, secret and nuknown to any other besides himself; therefore the care thereof belongs only to a *Chenifian Mussulman*, who has Religion and Faith."

He afterwards advis'd with the Lawyers of *Egypt*, who counselled him to bestow that charge on the Lawyer *Gabdol*, the son of *Gabdolsalem* the Schoolmaster. Others say he was called *Gait*, and that his Sirname was *Abulredad*. He was a very ancient man, who read the memorable actions and sayings of the Prophet in the great *Mosquey* of *Masre*, and who had been before a Schoolmaster teaching children. The *Mamunus* gave him the charge of Governour of the *Nilometer*, after it was fully built in the Year CCXLIV, and allotted him 7 Crowns of Gold monethly for his Pension, which has ever since been continued to his Successours. Others say it was *Mutavacquel* who caused it to be built. They say also that the *Coptites* had heretofore a *Nilometer* in the Castle of *Cire*. The *Romans* also had one in the Castle at *Babolsaguir*. *Gabdorrachaman* says after *Chaled*, who had it from *Iachi* the son of *Bequir;* "I came (said he) to the *Nilometer* of *Memphis* just as the Measurer entered into the *Fustata*, to carry thither the good news of the Augmentation of the *Nile*."

I have heard moreover (said the Author) a third story upon the cultivation of the Land of *Alphiom*, from *Mahumet* the Son of *Gali*, the Son of *Gabdol*, the Son of *Sachar* the *Teminian*, **A third story of *Alphiom*.** who spoke of it in these terms, sincerely citing the Author from whom he had it: "I have heard (said he) of a man who was of the Barbarians of *Egypt*, and well versed in the Affairs of his countrey, and its History, and its Antiquities, living in a village named *Phacat*, that he had found it in a book, that *Alphiom* was heretofore a Land full of Briars and Thorns, where nobody lived; and that about that time the daughter of a *Roman* Emperour having misbehaved her self, and her offence having been notorious all over the *Roman* Empire, even in the most remote Islands of the

Sea, her father resolved to put her out of all places under his Jurisdiction, and to send her to Sea. He put aboard with her her Mother, her Servants, and all her Retinue, and whatever belonged to her, and caused them to get out into the Main Sea; having beforehand ordered that Favourite of his whom he had entrusted with this affair, that when they met with violent Winds, he should dispose the Ships to sail into a countrey out of which they should never return. This Order was put in execution, and the Sails were hoised in the midst of the Sea, in the midst of a Tempest which blew every way, so that it carried away the Ships, and cast the Princess with those that accompanied her streight into *Egypt,* where she made up the *Nile* till she came to the *Manhi,* at a place where now *Lahon* is. There she went ashore, and got on horseback with some of her People to take a view of the Countrey, seeking a place where she might make her habitation, and set up her rest: for she had been told her Fathers will, and knew it was his design she should have perished in the Sea. After much riding she came to the place of *Alphiom,* and saw it covered with Briars, and Trees, and Pastures, and Standing Waters, and compass'd all about as it were with the Sea; after she had taken a full prospect of it, she returned to the Ship, and said to her Mother that she had found a place where they might settle themselves, and which they might cultivate for their subsistence; that there was not such another in the world, and that she had made choice of it for her aboad and retirement. 'Do what you please,' said her Mother to her. She therefore sent her Retinue before on Mules which they had with them in their Ships; then they took their way, and advanced as far as *Matartares,* which is in the midst of the City of *Alphiom,* remaining to this day. The water overflowed *Alphiom* from the *Manhi* when the *Nile* was at the highest; and when it was very low, the water ebbed from *Alphiom.* When therefore she saw the water gone back from *Alphiom,* she began to build Cities, to cut down what Trees were requisite, and to clear the ground of the Reeds, the Paper-plants, and the Tamarisk which grew there. Then she bethought her of a way to lay out the Money she had brought with her, and sent some of her Servants to the Villages, and to the Cities, to get people together; so that there came to her a great number of poor people, and necessitous Tradesmen, to whom she distributed wherewithall to subsist, and did them many favours, employing them in digging the Chanel of the *Manhi* as far as *Alphiem*. They wrought it, and began the design thereof; but they afterwards found they could not bring it to perfection, whereupon they gave it over. This is manifestly seen at this day by the tracks that are left of it. It is on the East side of the City of *Alphiom*. They raised the Bank of *Lahon*, that it might retain as much water as they stood in need of."

They relate moreover (says the Author) a fourth Story concerning the manner how the Land of *Alphiom* was peopled.

A fourth story of it.

Pharao (say these) commanded *Joseph* to reduce it, and proportionably to distribute the waters which flowed thence. *Joseph* did it, and so settled all, that it might last to the end of times upon the surface of the earth. The *Lahon* is at this day in that posture, save that *Abagon Gabdolmelic* the son of *Jezidus* has added something thereto, on that side which is towards the wall of the Sources. He also raised in the City of *Alphiom* a little Structure, which is of no use. The yearly Revenue of *Alphiom* was 365000 Crowns of Gold, without exaction, or injuring, or tyrannizing over any person. But since it hath been successively in the hands of several wicked Governours, who have laid Impositions according to their avarice, the Benediction hath departed from *Alphiom,* and the rest of the Countrey: the best cultivated places are grown desolate, most of the passages and villages were ruined, and its Revenues abated more and more. And yet if the Princes would cast their eyes on this Countrey, and cause it to be rpeopled, and provide for the observance of Justice and Equity therein, its Revenues would return to what they were before. But God knows what is concealed from Men.

As to *Joseph*'s Prison in *Egypt,* and the Benediction which God gives upon the Prayers made there, this is one of the Stories related thereof. There was heretofore Commander in *Egypt* the *Achesidian,* so called from the name of his Master *Abulchasam Gali* the son of

Joseph's Prison.

Achesides, who gave him the management of the Affairs of his Government, even during his life for a long time; so that after the death of *Abulchasam, Caphor* the *Achesidian* continued sole Governour of *Egypt,* and was put into the Government of that Province by the Prelate the *Mutigolell,* of the House of *Guebasus,* God shew him mercy, and generally all related to him; which he enjoyed alone, and without any Partner. *Caphor* died afterwards, but *Saphilmelic* the *Caid Guehar,* servant of the *Mugazzoldinill,* entered into *Egypt* even while he governed it, and obtained of him the Reversion of it. They say this *Caphor* (God shew him mercy) being one day very much troubled with a difficult and intricate business, went himself to the Lawyer and Doctor of *Egypt,* who was then *Abubeker* the son of *Chedad,* and having saluted him said thus to him: "I desire you to name me some place where Prayers are infallibly heard, and shew me in what manner I should pray for an Affair which hath happened to me, and hath already given me much disquiet." "Lord Commander (replied the Doctor) go your ways to *Joseph's* Prison, and say your Prayer over it with two Inclinations: if you say it in the Afternoon, it will be so much the better. After that read the Chapter of *Joseph* with a loud voice, and in an entire *Alcoran,* with your face turned towards *Meca,* standing, and your hands lifted up, and ask of God what you desire. For this kind of Prayer is experienced, ready to be heard and accepted: it is the Prayer of Necessity. I have known ancient *Egyptians* make use of it frequently."

Caphor departed, and did what the old man advised him, and God did the business for him within a week. The ancient *Egyptians,* as well the Doctors, and they that profess the knowledge of the sayings and actions of the Prophet, as before them, those of his company and retinue, have ever had recourse to that noble Prison, and there they called upon Almighty God for the accomplishment of their affairs, and their prayers were heard. *Moses,* who spoke with God, and his Brother *Aaron,* (Gods peace be with them both) even they have made their Prayers there, and obtained Divine Benedictions: for it is the Prison wherein their Uncle *Joseph* was detained; since *Moses* was the Son of *Gamran,* the Son of *Iaheb,* the Son of *Levi,* which *Levi* was *Ioseph's* Brother. They say that *Moses,* when he desired God to turn his indignation from the Inhabitants of *Egypt,* and to deliver them from the Locusts and the Frogs, and from the Deluge, and from the Bloud, made his Prayer over *Joseph's* Prison, as a place purposely set aside for the imploring of Gods mercy; to which the *Egyptians,* when they are visited with sterility and dearth, or persecution, or are disquieted by reason of any affair, run presently, and make their prayer there, which is certainly heard. *Jacob* (Gods peace be with him) added thereto the place of his She-Camel, where he made her kneel down that he might get off her back. Since the *Mussulman* Religion hath been observed, there is a Mosquey built in that place: it is under the Bank of Sand, upon which is the Prison. For *Jacob* (desirous to see the place where his Son had been Prisoner) rode thither on his She-Camel, and alighted at the place which is now called *Joseph's Mosquey,* and there prayed, and gave

The place of Jacob's Camel.

thanks to God for the favour he had done him, that he embraced his Son, and saw him again: then he went up to the Sand-Mount, and so to the Prison. JESUS the Son of *Mary* (Gods peace be with them both) did also visit that Prison. When he and his Mother were in *Egypt,* they there said their Prayer. Many of those who accompanied the Prophet entered into it; that is to say, the Fourscore who were in *Egypt* at the time of the Conquests, the first whereof was *Gamrou* the Son of *Gasus,* then his Son *Gabdol,* and *Zebirus* the Son of *Gavam,* and *Abuharirus,* and *Abudar,* and *Mecdad,* and the rest, (Gods be with them all;) nay some of them left their Prints upon the Roof of the Prison. This Prison is the place where *Joseph* sate when he interpreted the Dreams. On one side of the Prison there is a Vault, out of which *Gabriel* came down to him. *Zelicha* sate in that place (before he was more closely restrained, and that they had laid extraordinary commands upon

Zelicha, Joseph's Mistress.

him, and turned his face from the vault) that she might see him ever and anon from the upper part of her Castle: for the Prison served for a Tower to the gate of the Western House of *Gazizus,* which was then within the place of Pleasure. The King had two Houses; the Eastern, called *Zelicha's Gallery,* where is the Wall which remains to this day, opposite to the Caves: and the Western, where the Prison was, and belonged to the place of Pleasure. As to the Prayer which the Lawyer *Abubeker* (the Son of *Chedad)* taught *Caphor,* (Gods peace be with them both;) 'tis this:

***Caphor*'s Prayer.** "Great God, give thy Benediction to *Mahumet* and his Family, grant peace to *Mahumet* and to *Mahumet*'s Family, shew mercy on *Mahumet* and *Mahumets* Family, be propitious to *Mahumet* and to the Family of *Mahumet;* as thou hast given thy benediction and peace, and as thou hast been merciful, and as thou hast been propitious to *Abraham* and the Family of *Abraham.* Thou art praise-worthy, and glorious. Great God! O thou who hast saved thy Prophet *Joseph,* and hast delivered him out of the Dungeon, and out of Darkness, and hast made him to get happily out of prison, after the Devil had raised dissention between him and his brethren; who didst bring him to be embraced by his father after a long absence; who hast taken away the afflictions of his father the Prophet *Jacob,* and hast had compassion on the abundance of his Tears, and hast crowned his hope by causing him to see him after he had lost his sight, and hast restored him to him, as it were by a Miracle of his Prophecy; who hast heard his prayer, and done the business he desired of thee: Make haste to dissipate my affliction, and to facilitate to me the departure of my disquiet, do my business for me; facilitate my return to my own people, receive me into thy Sanctuary, deliver me out of my misfortunes, and out of my afflictions, as thou hast deliver'd thy Prophet *Joseph* out of his, after thou hadst afflicted him in this place, for the tryal of his patience; for the raising him to a high rank near thee, and for the increase of his reward. O Thou, who art he who dost compass the affairs of the faithful, who art the end of the desires of all that petition thee, and the Butt of their demands, who require any thing of thee, and the hope of those who seek a refuge, and the sanctuary of those who are in fear; who hearest the prayers of those who have need, and dost put a period to great afflictions! Bless *Mahomet* thy Apostle, and Lord of Men, and those of his holy Family, and those of his chosen Company, and his Wives, who are the Mothers of the Faithful, and those who follow them in well-doing to the day of judgement. Take me into thy custody, surround me with the Curtains of thy Throne, raise over me the Forts of thy Cittadels, spread over me the vail of thy protection, and turn not away thy eyes from me; give me not over into the tuition of any other, free me from the evil devices of thy creatures, favour me with the abundance of thy graces, and with that of thy goods whereof the use is allowed, through thy mercy, O most merciful of all the merciful. God give his Benedictions to our Lord *Mahumet*, and to those of his family, and to those of his company, and to his wives, and to those who follow them in well-doing to the day of judgment. Praise be to God the Lord of the world."

Megavius, the son of *Salichus* relates, as having learnt it of *Abuharirus*, God shew him mercy, that *Joseph*, Gods peace be with him, when he was brought into *Aegypt*, began to weep night and day, out of the grief it was to him, to be so far from his father and brethren; and that one night which he consecrated to God, and which he spent in prayer, he implor'd the assistance of God, and without any noise spoke thus to his Lord: "O Lord, thou hast brought me out of the Country which I love best of any in the world, do me good in this where I now am, and assist me therein with thy favours; cause me to be loving to the Inhabitants of these Provinces into which thou hast brought and conducted me, and in like manner cause them to love me: give me wherewithall to subsist therein happily and handsomely, and do me favour that I may not die till thou hast brought my Brethren and me together with joy and satisfaction, and put us into a capacity of enjoying the happiness of this world, and that of the other."

Joseph's Prayer.

After that, *Joseph* fell asleep, and saw in his dream some body, who said to him: "*Joseph*, God hath heard thy prayer; he will raise in thee an affection to the Country into which he hath brought thee, insomuch that there shall not be any other in the world, more pleasant to thee, as he hath alwaies made it amiable to those who have entred into it before thee; and in like manner he will render it amiable to those who shall enter into it after thee, for no body shall be desirous to go out of it, after he is once come into it. He will in like manner cause thee to be lov'd by its Inhabitants, and will make thee Master and Governour of it. He will also bring you together; thee and thy Father, and thy Brethren in the midst of thy reign and government, and will give thee joy and satisfaction. Take courage therefore upon this hope, and be jocund and chearful, and know, *Joseph,* that this Province is the Mother of Nations, and the support of Men, and that the Treasures and Wealth of the Earth are in it."

Joseph awaked thereupon extreamly glad and satisfi'd, and from that time advanc'd by degrees to the condition which God had promis'd him, alwaies hoping the accomplishment of the promises which he had made him, till that God brought hem together, him and his Father, and his Brethren. Ever since, *Ægypt* hath been ever lov'd and desir'd; no Forreigner comes into it, but is glad to continue there, and departs thence, but he regrets it and desires to return into it again. After God had brought him to Reign, and brought them together, him, and his Father and his Brethren, in the flower of his glory, power, and grandeur, he humbled himself before God, and abstain'd from the goods of the world, aspiring to those which are with God, and said, according to what God himself relates of him by the mouth of his Prophet *Mahumet,* Gods peace and mercy be with him, in his glorious Book: "*My* Lord, *you have brought me to Reign, and have given me the knowledge of interpreting obscure discourses; O Creator of the Heavens and the Earth. You are my Protector in this world, and in the other give me the grace to die a* Mussulman, *and bring me into the company of the Vertuous.*" God granted him all that; God bless him and his holy Fathers.

Abumuchammed the *Achemimian,* the *Dyer,* God have mercy on him, related to me at *Masre,* what follows, sayes the Author: "I went often," said he, "to the Country of *Gize* about some affairs I had there, and some debts I was to receive from certain Labourers of those parts, so that I saw the *Pyramids* at a distance; but the trouble

The Pyramids.

and disquiet I was in proceeding from my affairs, permitted me not to go to them, nor to come nearer them, to consider them at leisure, and to contemplate their structure, and the exquisite artifice of their Fabrick. I was acquainted with, and much esteem'd, the Prelate of the great *Mosquey* of that Country, so that one night I took up my lodging at his house, and discover'd to him my thoughts concerning the *Pyramids,* telling him, that I had always been so taken up with my affairs, that I had not as yet gone so far to consider them, but that I had a great desire to see them, and to contemplate the structure thereof, and the excellency of the artifice employ'd therein. He thereupon spoke thus to me: 'Brother, if these *Pyramids* were in *China,* or at the extremities of the West, those who should hear talk of them, would have the curiosity to go thither to see them, and to consider the admirable structure thereof; what therefore ought they to do who are here in the Country where they are, and so near them?' My Father told me, that he had seen *Magedolmelic Macherir* the blind man, who got the *Alcoran* read to him at the gate of the Western Castle, Gods mercy on

Macherir the Blind man.

him, in the time of the Prelate *Mustagalibemrillus,* who had seen him; I say, at these *Pyramids,* attended by an *Ethiopian* Youth, who led him by the hand, and that the Youth having brought him upon the *Pyramid* which lies Eastward, he felt the graving of it with his hand, and what was written upon it, and admir'd it, praising and giving thanks to God continually for the knowledge he had inspir'd his servants withall, and the excellency of their workmanship and *Geometry*. My Father saluted him, and spoke thus to him; "'O Lord, you put your self to much trouble, and take a great deal of pains to get up and down this Pyramid." "O Brother," reply'd he, "to travel up and down the Country, and to consider the tracks of ancient Nations, and past ages, is one of those things which are recomended to us, that those who want examples may thereby find some for their instruction, and that the sloathful and sleepy may therein meet with what may awake them out of their slumber, and oblige them to consider the Kingdom of the Heavens and the Earth, and the Miracles, and prodigious things which God hath placed therein. These Pyramids are one of the most miraculous things of any in *Egypt,* after the *Nile.* For as to the *Nile,* its flowings and ebbings depend on a wisedom known only to him who gives it its course, and obliges it to do its duty; who commands it to encrease, and it obeys; and who causes it to fall, after it hath acquitted it self of what people needed from it. What is there more admirable then these prodigies? For my part, I am a poor man, who have lost my sight, and whose curiosity can reach only those miracles and rarities, which may be learnt by the ear. But who comes it, that those who see well, who have leasure, and live near these miracles, have not the curiosity to divert themselves in the contemplation thereof?"

"'He thereupon took me by the hand, and recited these verses to me. *"Pray unto him who hath liv'd upon the Mount, to dictate unto thee the History of himself, and cause him not to weep, unless it be with my tears. I cannot see remote countries with my eyes, but it may be I shall see them by the means of my ears."* Whereupon he fell a weeping, so that he made me weep also, and said to me: "O Brother know that the sighs of the poor blind man will never end in this world, and that they will not cease, till he hath casted death, and that God hath promis'd him, that if he patiently endure the affliction of his blindness, and loss of his sight, and shall have taken it as coming from God, and chearfully accepted it, he will justifie him, and bring him into Paradise. For the blind man is dead among the living. The Law of God commands a man to salute him; it is an act of faith, to eat with him; it is an Oblation to God, to sit down with him; 'tis a merit of reward to discourse with him; 'tis a thing of obligation to give him an almes; he who takes him by the hand in his necessity obtains the remission of his sins." Then he said further to me: "Know that what oblig'd me to take the pains to come to this place, was somewhat told me by a certain Scholar while we were together in the Colledge.

"'Twas of his father that he spoke to me, and he was of that Country of *Gize.* "My father," said he, "told me, that while he was a young man, he went and came many times night and day by these Pyramids, his affairs obliging him thereto; and that he and some other young men about his age went up on the top of them, and sometimes into them, without any other design then to divert themselves. 'One day among others,' said this father to his son, according to what he added, 'about noon being mounted on a beast which I had, as I kept along my direct way, passing near these Pyramids, I saw a company of *Cavaliers,* mounted some on Horses, and others on Camels, and some people a foot marching along with them, as it were in a Procession about the Pyramids. Whereupon thought I to to my self, Who are those that make a Procession about the Pyramids now at noon? Is it not for some accident newly happen'd in the City? I thereupon made towards them, so that I came pretty near them, and look'd upon them very earnestly. But I found, as I view'd them at a nearer distance, that they had neither the stature nor meen of ordinary men, and I made the same judgement of their Horses and their Camels. Which oblig'd me to recommend my self to God, after which I saluted them, and they return'd my salutation, and spoke thus to me; "Be of good courage, thou shalt have no harm. We are a company of *Mussulmans,* of the number of the *Dæmons,* who believe in God and in his Prophet. When the *Dæmons* return a mans salutation, he may believe himself safe enough as to them. When therefore thou shalt meet with creatures which thou thinkest not to be men, salute them, for if they salute thee again, they will be faithful, if they do not return thy salutation, they will not be faithful; it will therefore concern thee to recommend thy self to God, that he may preserve thee from them; for by that means it will not be in their power to hurt thee."

Mussulman Dæmons.

""""After that I saw among them a *Dæmon* whom they honoured much, and whom they acknowledg'd as it were for their Protector and Superiour, to whom one of them spoke thus. "See you the beauty and the excellency, and the workmanship of that Structure, and of that Architecture, the solidity of those buildings, and the goodness of their situation?" "This," reply'd he, "'is an effect of their wisdom, who inhabited the land before us, who were mightier then we, and fignaliz'd themselves, by more noble marks, then we can do, upon the earth. I had heard what the

The Pyramids. ancients said of these Pyramids, and was desirous to see and consider them my self before my death, should we now at the time we live in, attempt the making of such works as these, we should not compass them, even though men joyn'd with us to carry on the work. Nay, though we should content our selves with the building of but one Pyramid, we should not be able to do it; what pain therefore would it be to make as many as there are here?" After that they departed as it were in order to their return, and one of them bid me *Adieu,* and spoke thus to me; "O man, endeavour to forbear walking abroad at noon; rather sleep at mid-day, for the Devils do not sleep at that time."

""""Now this is it that obliged me to come to these Pyramids, which are such Miracles of Workmanship, that the Dæmons themselves cannot make the like. Why shall I not feel them at least with my hand? Besides, here is a Youth who represents things so well to me, that I comprehend them as if I saw them my self: I thank God who guides my Imagination so well.""""

We find in the Book of the Lives of great and illustrious persons, who have flourished in several times, that *Masre* (God preserve it) was anciently called *Babelain,* and that that name had been given it in regard that *Babel* being heretofore the seat of the Empire of *Gueraca* and *Syria,* when the Kingdom of *Masre* came to be great and famous in the world the *Coptites* called it *Babelain,* pretending by that name to raise the lustre of its State, and to exalt the glory and dignity of its Empire: as if they would say, the ancient *Babel* was but one *Babel,* and that *Masre* was *Babelain,* that is to say, two *Babels.* Whence it came, that after the *Romans* got to be Masters of *Syria,* they said the Land of *Egypt* is *Babylon,* and made great account of that Province by reason of the conveniences they had thence by Sea and by Land; so that that name continued to it. Then upon its being taken by the *Mussulmans* under the Reign of *Omar,* (Gods peace be with him) by the conduct of *Gamrou* the son of *Gasus,* (Gods mercy on him) an *Arabian* Poet made Verses, wherein he acknowledged the favour God had done them in that conquest, and the abundance and variety of good things and wealth which they had acquired by that victory. The subject of those Verses was, that *Quisias* the son of *Caltham,* one of the Children of *Som,* (Gods mercy on him) came from *Syria* to *Masre* with *Gamron* the Son of *Gasus,* and entered into it with 100 men of his Nation, bringing their equipage on horses; which men he commanded, having belonging to him 50 Servants and 30 Horses. *Gamrou* and the *Mussulmans* being afterwards resolved to besiege the Castle, *Quisias* chose a place where he and his men might continue, and caused his Tent to be pitched there, according to the relation of *Abugamrou Mahumet* the Son of *Joseph,* and aboad there during the whole Siege of the Castle, till God brought it into their power. After that *Quisias* was with *Gamrou* at *Alexandria,* leaving his people and his baggage in that place; and after *Alexandria* had also been taken by the *Mussulmans* as *Gamrou* was returning to *Masre,* having imposed on the *Alexandrians* the Tribute they were to pay, and signed the Articles of their Accommodation: *Quisias* returned also to his Quarters at *Masre,* and lodg'd there still. The *Mussulmans* marked Lodgings for themselves, and *Gamrou* caused his own to be marked opposite to that heap of Sand where *Quisias* had taken up his Post. Then the *Mussulmans* had a Council about the building of a Mosquey, where they might meet together, and writ concerning it to the Commander of the Faithful, *Omar,* (Gods peace be with him) who returned this answer; "I have received the news of the resolution which you have taken up all together for the building of a Mosquey, where you may celebrate the Friday, and make your Assemblies. It is no doubt a thing necessary for you, and you follow in that the example of your Prophet, Gods peace and mercy be upon him. For the first mark whereby he began to signalize the *Mussulman* Religion and the first foundation upon which he would settle it, was the building of his own Mosquey in the place of his Retreat. Assemble therefore hereupon your Commanders, and take counsel of your ancients, who are Companions of the Apostle of God, Gods peace and mercy be with them, for the benediction, of God is in the Ancients. What they shall resolve on with a general consent, approve it,

Quisias the son of Caltham.

O Gamron, and oppose it not. For the assembly of the Council brings the mercy of God, who protects that Nation, out of the kindness he hath for his Prophet, Gods peace and mercy be with him. Through the grace and mercy of God, they will never agree about a thing wherein there is any errour. God keep you in union, and prosper your affairs, and settle you in the possession of your Conquests, and assist both you and me with his graces, and bless *Mahumet* and his family."

The *Mussulmans* having seen *Omar*'s answer, Gods peace and mercy be with him, held a Council concerning the building of the Mosquey, and found it might be conveniently built on the place where *Quisias* the son of *Colthom* was lodg'd. *Gamrou* sent for him, and ask'd his advice, saying; "*O Abugabdorrachaman,* I will take up a lodging for you instead of this, where you please to have it." Whereupon *Quisias* spoke thus: "I have already told you, O ye *Mussulmans,* who are hear assembled, that this habitation pleases me well, and that it is mine, but I bestow it with all my heart on God and the *Mussulmans.*"

He therefore quitted that place, and lodg'd with those of his Nation, who were the children of *Som,* and took up his Quarters among them. Whereupon *Abucainan* the son of *Magamar,* the son of *Rabagui,* the *Nachesian,* in memory of those adventurers, and to honour these Victories, made the ensuing verses: "*And we had the good fortune to Conquer* Babylon, *where we have pitch'd upon booty in abundance for* Omar *and for God. The good man* Quisias, *the son of* Calthom, *quitted and delivered up his habitation and the lodging which belonged to him upon the divine intreaty. All those who shall do their devotions in our structure, will know with the inhabitants of* Masre *what I say, and will publish it.*" *Abumansor* the *Balavian,* Gods mercy on him, made these Verses upon the same subject, wherein he speaks of *Gabdorrachaman,* the son of *Quisias,* the son of *Calthom,* Gods peace be with him; "*And thy Father quitted and deliver'd up his habitation to the people of prayer and adoration.*" *Lithus,* the son of *Sagad,* Gods mercy on him, a Lawyer of *Masre,* speaks thus of the ancient great Mosquey of that City; "*Our Mosquey was only Gardens and Vineyards.*" *Abugamrou,* the son of *Serragus,* sayes this of it, which he had from *Saguidus,* who had it from the Ancients of his time; "The place," saith he, "of our great Mosquey of *Masre,* was heretofore only gardens and groves of Palmes, but the *Mussulmans* got it, and caused a Mosquey to be built there for their assemblies, (Gods peace be with them all). *Guemarus* the son of *Zebirus* the Cryer, sayes his Father spoke thus of it: "I have heard," said he, "our Ancients, of whom some had been present at the Conquest, who spoke thus: 'There were fourscore of the Companions of the Prophet of God, (God's peace and mercy be with them) present at the foundation of the Mosquey of *Masre, Zebirus* the son of *Gavam, Mecdad* the son of *Asouad, Guebad,* the son of *Samet, Abuldarda, Phedal, Gamron, Gaqueb,* and the rest, as well of the number of those who came for refuge, as of that of the Protectors, (Gods peace be with them all.)'" *Jezibus:* the son of *Chebib,* speaks thus of it. "Our Mosquey was founded by four of the Companions of the Prophet, Gods peace and mercy be with them, *Abudar, Abunasre, Mahumet* the son of *Gerou* the *Zebirian,* and *Manbehe* the son of *Derar.*" *Gabidol* the son of *Gegafur* speaks thus of it in these terms: "Our Temple was raised by *Guebad,* the son of *Samet,* and by *Raphecus,* the son of *Malichus,* who were two Captains of the Protectors, Gods mercy on them." *Abudaoud* saith, that *Gamrou,* the son of *Gasus,* sent *Rabigas* the son of *Sergil,* and the son of *Galcamas* the *Carsian,* the *Guedavian,* to determine on which side should be the Front of the Mosquey, and that he spoke thus to them; "Go you and stand on the top of the Mountain, when the Sun is ready to set, and when there shall be one half of it under the Horizon, do you turn so as that it may be on your Eye-brows, and take with all the exactness you can, the true side on which the Temple ought to be turned. I pray God to assist you in the doing of it."

The Front of a Mosquey.

They did what he had commanded them. "I have heard," says *Lithus,* (Gods mercy on him) "that *Gamrou* the son of *Gasus* went up to the Mountains, and exactly observed the time, and the shade of the Sun setting, till the side on which the front of the Temple should be turn'd was agreed upon. *Guemarus* related to me, that he had heard his Father say, that *Gamrou* the son of *Gasus* said to his Companions, 'Turn the front of the Mosquey towards the East, that it may be right opposite to *Meca.*' It was turned (said he) very much towards the East; but after that *Corras* the son of *Coris* made it incline a little toward the South." "I have heard (saith *Masgab)* the son of *Abuchebib,* who spoke thus upon these words of the All-mighty and All-good God, *'We shall see on which side thou wilt turn thy Face towards the Heaven, and we shall appoint thee a Situation which thou shalt be pleased withall.'* "This Situation (saith *Jezidus)* which the Apostle of God (Gods peace and mercy be with him) observed in his Prayers, and which All-mighty God commanded him to comply withall, consisted in having the face turned towards the Chanel; and it is the Situation of the *Egyptians,* and of the Inhabitants of the Western parts." "I have heard the same *Abuchebib,*" added *Masgab,* "read that passage after another manner, putting the first person instead of the second, thus; *'And we will appoint thee a Situation, which we shall be pleased withall.'* One of the Protectors saith, that *Gabriel* came to the Apostle of God (Gods peace and mercy be with him) and said unto him; 'Dispose the Situation of thy Mosquey so as thou maist have thy face turned towards the square Temple.' Then he made his draughts upon all the Mountains which were between him and the square Temple, and so he drew the Platform of his Mosquey, having his face turned towards the square Temple, which happen'd to be the Chanel side." *Malicus* affirms that the Front of the Mosquey of the Prophet of God (Gods peace and mercy be with him) is Situated opposite to the Chanel. Several Authors relate, that in the Mosquey of *Gamrou,* the son of *Gasus,* there was no vaulted Upper-room, nor in that built by *Muslemas,* nor in that built by *Gabdolgueziz,* the son of *Merouan;* and that the first who made an Upper-arched room was *Corras,* the son of *Masquin.* They say the son of *Serich* speaks thus of it: "In the great Mosquey, which *Gamrou* the son of *Gasus* built; there was no Arch, that is, no Arched Upper-room." *Saguidus* the son of *Serich* speaks also of it in these terms; "*Abusaguid* related this to me. 'The *Chemirian,* who is the most aged of those whom I have met, said to them: I have found this Mosquey where you assemble your selves, and which was built by *Gam-*

rou, the son of *Gasus,* fifty Cubits in length, and thirty in breadth.'" *Gamer* the son of *Omar,* the son of *Chebib,* the Crier, speaks thus of it; "*Gamrou* the son of *Gasus* spoke to us, and made a Street which compassed the Mosquey on all sides; then he made two Gates opposite to the House of *Gamrou,* the son of *Gasus,* and two Gates on the East side, and two Gates on the West side, so that when the people went out of the little Street of the *Lampe,* they found the East-corner of the Mosquey opposite to the West-corner of the House of *Gamrou,* the son of *Gasus;* and that before they had taken out of *Gamrou*'s House, what was since taken out. The length of the Mosquey, from the front to the opposite end was equal to the length of *Gamrou*'s House. The Roof on the outside was very flat. In Summer the people sate all about in the spacious place which was at the entrance." *Abusalich* speaks thus of it; "*Lithus* said to me one day, 'can you tell what distance there was between the Mosquey built by *Gamrou,* and his House?' 'No,' said I. 'Our Ancients told me (reply'd he) that there were seven Cubits, and that before they took out of *Gamrou*'s House, what was since taken, and made part of the Mosquey. This shews that the Eastern Gate was opposite to the great House of *Gamrou.*' The son of *Lahig* relates it to us as a thing he had learnt of the son of *Habir,* that *Abutemim,* the *Chisanian,* had said to him, that he had heard *Gamrou* the son of *Gasus* speaking in these terms: "One of the Companions of the Apostle of God (Gods peace and mercy be with him) told me he had heard the Prophet, (Gods peace and mercy be with him) speak thus; 'The All-mighty and All-good God commands you one Prayer besides the ordinary ones; say it in the intervall there is from the Evening Prayer to the break of day.'"

Abunasre the *Gopharian* related it, and *Abutemim* speaks of it thus; "As we sate down together, *Abudar* and I, *Abudar* took me by the hand, and we went together to *Abunasre,* whom we met at the Gate, which is on the side of *Gamrou*'s House, where *Abudar* spoke to him thus; 'O *Abunasre,* have you heard the Apostle of God (Gods peace and mercy be with him) speak in these terms? "God hath yet enjoined you a Prayer; say it in the intervall between the Evening and betimes in the Morning."' He repeated this to him three times, and he always answered, 'Yea.'" *Jachi* the son of *Salich,* relates what follows, as having it from *Gadras,* who had it from his Father, and he from *Gamer* the son of *Omar.* "*Muslemas* (said he) caused to be made in the great Mosquey, four Chappels at the four corners of it; for he first put them there, and they were not there before. He also was the first who spread it with Mat, for before that it was only strew'd with Gravel." After him *Gabdolgueziz,* the son of *Merouam,* the son of *Chacam,* caused somewhat to be done therein, according to the relation of *Gamer,* the son of *Omar,* the son of *Chebib,* the *Raguinian,* who affirms that *Gabdolgueziz,* the son of *Merouan* quite demolish'd the great Mosquey, and that he augmented it on the West-side, so that he left between it and the House of *Sand,* and the House of *Gerou*'s Son, and the others, but a small Street, which is now called the *Pav'd Street,* and brought into it the spacious place, which was on the North-side; but on the East-side he had no place to enlarge it. This was done in the year 79. As to the augmentations made in the great ancient Mosquey, after the building of it, by *Gamrou* the son of *Gasus,* it is to be observed, that *Gamrou* did this work after his return from *Alexandria,* to the place of his Tent, and that he had taken *Masre* in the Moneth *Mucharram,* in the twentieth year after the Prophet's Retreat, whom God favour with his most excellent Benedictions. *Abusaguid* the *Chemirian* speaks of it also; "I have found that that Mosquey, where you assemble your selves, was built by *Gamrou,* fifty Cubits in length, and thirty in breadth. After him *Muslemas* the son of *Muchalled* made some enlargements in it, under the Reign of *Megavius,* the son of the *Abusophian,* in the year 35. Then afterwards *Gabdolgueziz,* the son of *Merouan,* in the year 79. and after him *Corras,* the son of *Serich,* upon the account of the *Valide* the son of *Gabdolmelic.* This last would needs demolish what *Gabdolgueziz* had built, and afterwards completed his building. He gave the ovesight of these works to *Jachi* the son of *Chandelas,* and above him to *Gamer* the son of *Levi.* He quite demolished the Mosquey, so that the people met on *Friday* in an-

The augmentations of the Mosquey of Masre.

other place, till the building was finished. He put up the Seat for Orations in the great Mosquey, in the year 94. They say there is not in the World any one handsomer and nobler then this, after the Seat of the Prophet of God, Gods peace and mercy be with him. After that, there were enlargements made by *Salich*, the son of *Gali*, the son of *Gabdol*, the son of *Guebas*, upon the account of the Commander of the Faithful *Abulguebas*, who added behind the Mosquey four Pillars. There were also some made by *Gabdol*, the son of *Tahar*, the son of *Ghasan*, the Overseer, under the Commander of the Faithful." *Gabdol* says this of it, as having it from his Father; "*Abutahar* came from *Alexandria*, and entered into *Fustata*, which is *Masre*, where he constituted Judge *Guise*, the son of the *Moncader*, and added to the Mosquey part of the House of *Gamrou* the son of *Gasus*. The son of *Remath* added thereto the House of *Gabidol*, the son of *Chareth*, the son of *Gerou*, and the House of *Gagelan*, the freed Servant of *Omar*, the son of *Chettab*, (Gods peace be with him) and the House of the *Phadal*. The *Phadal*, the son of *Tahar*, went out of it accordingly on a *Tuesday*, five days before the expiration of the Moneth *Regebe*, in the year 212. After him *Abubeker Mahumet*, the son of *Gabidol*, the son of *Chareth*, the son of *Masquin*, enlarged it on the side of the spacious place, and to that end took the Gate, and the Mint-house, with what was adjoyning thereto, as far as the Western Wall of the Mosquey, which so enlarged the spacious place, that the Mosquey was square. He added thereto also a Pillar, which is that on the South-side. He began to demolish and to build on *Thursday* the fourth of the Moneth of *Regebe*, in the year 357. and dy'd before he had finish'd his design; but his son *Gali*, the son of *Mahumet*, had his charge after his death, and completed the enlargements which he had begun; so that the people did their Devotions there after *Wednesday* the 23. of the Moneth *Ramadan*, in the year 358. The *Phadal* the son of *Guebas* told me what follows; 'I ask'd (said he) the Architect, named *Gali*, the *Chemirian*, who had the charge of that Structure; and he told me that what was taken out of the Mint-house towards the enlargement of the spacious Place is nine Cubits in length, according to the great measure.'" *Sophian* the son of *Gabdol* says, citing for Author *Naphegus*, the son of

History read in the Mosquey

Othman, that there was no History recited in the Mosquey in the time of the Apostle of God, (Gods peace and mercy be with him, nor in the time of *Abubeker, Omar, Othman,* or *Gali,* (Gods peace be with them all) and that practise began not till under the Reign of *Megavius* the son of *Abusophian.* The son of *Lahigus* saith, citing for Author *Abuchei,* that *Gali* (Gods peace be with him) went to his Devotion before day, making imprecations against some of his enemies; and that it being related to *Megavius,* he appointed a man to recite the History after the break of Day, and after Sun-set, and to pray God for him, and the Inhabitants of *Syria;* and thence began (saith he) the recital of History. *Abugamrou* hath related to us, citing for Author *Meguirus,* that the first who did his Devotions in the morning was *Gali,* and they say he did not that but out of a reflection that he had a War to prosecute.

The green Tables of the Mosquey of Masre.

We will add here a Copy of what is writen upon the green Tables in the ancient great Mosquey of *Masre.* The Writer was *Abulcasem Moses,* the son of *Guise,* the son of *Moses,* the son of *Muadi* the Writer, God. All-mighty be merciful to him.

"In the Name of God Gracious and Merciful; God hath declared that there is no other God but he (till he says) in Justice. 'There is no other God but the true God alone, without Associate. He gives Life and Death, and he can do all things. 'Tis he who hath sent his Apostle with good conduct, and the true Religion;' and the rest of the Verse. 'The Messias will not disdain;' and the rest of the Verse. Great God, give thy Benediction to *Mahumet* thy Servant and Prophet, grant him peace; make him the most honoured of thy Creatures before thee, and the most cherish'd by thee, and and the most Powerful in favour about thee, and the nearest in dignity to thee. Great God, hear the Prayers which *Mahumet* makes to thee for his Nation, and cause his People to descend into his Fish-pool, without confusion and without affliction. *Gabdol* the Strong, Commander of the Faithful, hath caused this Mosquey to be augmented and enlarged;

great God, give thy Benediction to the Commander of the Faithful, thou and thy Angels, encrease his reward, and make him one of thy greatest Servants in happiness; make him one of the Companions of *Mahumet* (Gods peace and mercy be with him) in Paradise; assist him to govern well what he hath under his jurisdiction of thy Servants, and of thy Provinces, by making him thy Lieutenant; and cause his Subjects to enjoy the happiness of good conduct in safety and assurance. He who had the oversight of the Structure was *Corras* the son of *Serich;* and the time wherein it was finished, is the Moneth *Ramadan,* in the ninety second year of the Blessed Retreat."

I have heard *Abugamrou* speak thus: "The first who made Arched Upper-rooms was *Omar,* the son of *Gabdolgueziz,* (Gods peace and mercy be with him) in the hundreth year; and the Mosqueys were made in that manner after him, having been before onely without any such Room. The first of the Prelates who caused the Benediction and the glorification of the Name of God to be pronounced by Criers after him, was the Prelate of *Chasina,* whose Son is now known under the name of the Son of *Gali* the Prelate. Before that, the Prelates only pronounced that Benediction to the People." I have heard him speak in these terms: "These Pillars of Wood which are in the Court, were erected the same year that the Chanel was made. Before that the Veils were in the midst of the Seeling of the great Mosquey." 'Tis related that in the Reign of the *Mamanus* there were Coffers in the great Mosquey, wherein was put what remained of the portions of the Poor and Indigent, of what they gather'd who walked up and down the High-ways, of all the other Collections which were made. These Coffers or Chests were opened on the *Friday,* and they call'd with a loud voice such as would accept of those Alms; but it seldom happened that any came to receive them. Then they call'd him who had gathered them, and he answered in these terms; "The Charities are come into the Coffers, they shall never return to me; I leave them to the All-mighty and All-good God." The *Nilometer* was built of the remainder of these Almes; there being not any would receive them in the time of the *Mamunus,* Gods mercy on him. One of the Grandees of *Egypt* (God shew him mercy) related to me, that heretofore in the *Lampe*-street in *Masre,* on the Festival day, after the great Feast of the Moneth *Ramadan,* they set Kettles full of Flesh, and Baskets full of Bread, and that they called with a loud voice such as had need thereof, as they call people to Water on the High-ways; and that it happened sometimes the greatest part remained there all Night upon the place, so few would take of it. The remainder was carried to the Prisoners, and they answered, "We have enough to live upon, thanks be to God." The Land of *Egypt* was then the most plentiful of any in the world, the most Populous, and the best cultivated, and where there was more convenience of Habitation and Subsistance. The *Masich* relates in his Annals, and others affirm also, that the *Egyptians,* when they saw the *Nile* at the highest, gave Almes, released Slaves, cloath'd Orphans, relieved Widows, and such as were destitute of Succour, out of their thankfulness to God, for the kindness he did them in raising the course of the *Nile* to its height.

Pharao's Castle. They relate that *Pharaoh,* after he grew Proud, and Insolent, and Impious, commanded a Castle to be built on the descent of Mount *Mactam;* and that his Visier *Haman,* according to this order, got workmen together from all parts of *Egypt;* so that there were a hundred and fifty thousand Architects, with what Trades-men, Handycraftsmen, and Labourers were requisite. He caused Brick and Mortar to be made, Timber to be felled, and Nails to be made; then they began their Building, and raised it so high, that never any had done the like before; for the Masons were no longer able to stand on their Feet to work. But the All-mighty and All-good God about Sun-set sent *Gabriel* (Gods peace be with him) who smote the Castle with his Wing, and cleft it into three pieces, one whereof fell on *Pharaoh*'s Army, where it kill'd a thousand Men; another fell into the Sea, and appeared there like a high Mountain; and the third fell into the Western Land. There was not so much as one of the *Coptites* who wrought within it saved, they all perish'd. They relate that thereupon *Pharaoh* was so proud, as to cast an Arrow at Heaven; God willing to try him, returned his Arrow to him all bloody; Whereupon he cry'd out, "I have killed *Moses*'s God." God is infinitely above what impious men can do; he does what he pleases with his Servants. God therefore at that very time sent *Gabriel,* who did to the Castle as we have related.

One of those who were impious, and proud, and arrogant in the Land of *Egypt,* was *Caron* the Cup-bearer; He was an *Israelite,* Cousin-german to *Moses,* (Gods peace be with him) for *Caron* was the son of *Jashar,* the son of *Caheb,* and *Moses* was the son of *Gamran,* the son of *Caheb.* Others say *Moses* was *Caron*'s Sisters son; he was called *Caron* the Bright, by reason of the beauty of his Face. He was the most diligent of the Children of *Israel* in the reading of *Moses*'s Law, but he became a Hypocrite, as the *Samerian* was, and said; "Since the Prophecy belonged to *Moses,* and the Sacrifice, and the Oblation, and the knowledge of the Law to *Aaron,* what remains there for me?"

Caron the Wealthy, who is *Corah.*

They relate that *Moses* having brought the Children of *Israel* through the Sea, gave *Caron* a Commission to interpret the Law, and to collect the Offerings, and made him one of the Chiefs. The Offerings belonged then to *Moses,* but he bestowed them on his Brother, whereat *Caron* was troubled, and envy'd them both, and spoke thus to them; "Behold now the command is come absolutly into your hands, and I have nothing to do with the affairs of the Children of *Israel;* How long shall I suffer this?" "It is God," reply'd *Moses,* "who thus disposes of things." "I will not believe it," reply'd *Caron,* "if you do not confirm it to me by a Miracle."

Then *Moses* commanded the Children of *Israel* to come all to him, every one with his Rod; then he ty'd all those Rods together, and cast them into the Tent, where God ordinarily revealed his Will to him. They kept a Guard about the Rods all night, and the next morning they found *Aaron*'s Rod shaking with the Wind, covered all over with green Leaves. That Rod was made of a Branch of Almond-trees.

"This is no more miraculous (said *Caron)* then what the Magicians daily perform."

He became thence forward more impious then before, more wicked, more envious, and more malicious against *Moses* and *Aaron,* as God affirms in his Book, when he saith, "Caron *was of the People of* Moses, *but he was unjust towards them.*" Injustice here signifies a persecution without any cause, and a malicious and irrational Dispute. Others affirm that *Pharao* appointed *Caron* to govern the Children of *Israel,* and that he treated them injuriously and tyrannically. Tyranny (they say) proceeds from greatness, that is, from the eminence and advantage which any one hath over others. The advantage he had over them was grounded on his great Wealth, and the multitude of his children. He made (say they) his Garments larger by a span then theirs; His Keys (say they) that is the Keys of his Store-houses, were carried by sixty Mules; Every Store-house had its Key, and every Key was but a Finger long; they were of Leather. Some affirm, expounding that passage of the Book of the All-mighty and All-good God, where it is said of him, *"I have not received it, but according to the knowledge which is within me;"* that he was the best skilled of his time in the Law of *Moses.* On the contrary, others affirm he was skilled in Chemistry; *Saguid* the son of *Musib* says,

Moses's Chemistry. that *Moses* had the Science of *Chemistry,* and that he taught a third purt of it to *Josuah,* the son of *Nun,* a third to *Caleb,* the son of *Jethnas,* and a third to *Caron,* but that *Caron* served the other two so well, that he learnt the whole Science from them both, and that afterwards he took Lead and Copper, and changed it into pure Gold. Others affirm that *Moses* taught his Sister Chemistry, inasmuch as his Devotion made him despise Gold, and that his Sister taught it *Caron,* who was her Husband. They relate that *Moses* said, it was a provision for the life of this World, and that he had no need thereof, because it was a perishable thing, and far distant from the truth, which is All-mighty God, and that he quitted what was perishable, which his Devotion permitted him not to desire, and satisfy'd himself with what was neer All-mighty God. They say that *Caron* went abroad one day on a white Mule he had, covered with a Foot-cloth of Purple, and a Golden Saddle, accompany'd by four thousand young Men, and three hundred beautiful young Maids, clad in Silk, and set out with Jewels and Ornaments of great value, and divers colours; so that he had marching on his right hand three hundred young men, and on his left three hundred young maids. Others say he went abroad on Horse-back attended by ninety thousand Servants Men and Maids, who belonged to him, young men and young maids all Marriageable. They relate that he gave very reproachful words to *Moses,* and the Children of *Israel,* priding himself in his great Wealth, *Moses* taking much at his hands for Kindred sake, and not willing to be incensed against him, till the Ordinance for the payment of Tiths came down. Then *Moses* made an Agreement with *Caron,* that of a thousand Crowns of Gold he should pay one, and of a thousand Drachmes one. But his Soul grew the more Covetous, by reason of the great quantity of Gold and Silver which he had, after he had counted it, and found so much. He thereupon assembled the Children of *Israel,* and began to make Speeches to them, and spoke to them in these terms; "*Moses* has hitherto dealt with you as he pleased himself, and now he would take away your goods." "You are our Lord and Master (reply'd they) command us to do what you think good." "We must (said he) corrupt such a one, naming a woman of a lewd life, and induce her to calumniate *Moses,* so as that he may be suspected to have had some dealings with her, that the Children of *Israel* may be put out of the good opinion they have of him, and have an aversion for him, and at last quite forsake him."

They promised that debauch'd woman a 1000. Crowne of gold; others say a Basin full of gold. Then the day of one of their Festivals being come, *Moses* stood up to speak to them; and after he had praised God, and given thanks, he spoke thus; "O ye Children of *Israel,* God commands you & me also, that if any one among us be a Thief, we should put him away from us; if any one commit Fornication, and be not married, we should punish him with the Whip, and if he be married, we should stone him." "And if you your self have committed those crimes, O *Moses,*" said *Caron.* "Yes," reply'd *Moses,* "though it were my self." "Certainly" reply'd *Caron,* "the Children of *Israel* believe that you have sinned with such a woman," naming the debauched woman.

Moses having heard these words sent for the woman, and charged her by him who had divided the Sea, and sent the Law from Heaven, to declare the truth. Then God of his mercy, touched the womans heart, and she spoke thus: "By the true God, those who say it speak an untruth; but true it is, that *Caron* and his people have promised me a reward if I testify'd that you had sinned with me, O great Prophet, who have spoken to God."

Then *Moses* fell down to the ground, and worshipped God weeping, and made this Prayer to him; "O Lord, if I am thy Apostle, avenge me, for it is impossible for me to endure those who have not thy fear before their eyes." And God revealed his will to him, speaking thus: "Command the Earth to do what thou desirest, and by my permission it shall obey thee."

Moses lift up his head, and said to the people; "O ye Children of *Israel*, God hath sent me to *Caron* as he sent me to *Pharao;* let such of you as are of his party stand near him."

They all withdrew from *Caron,* save onely two men, who continued obstinate in their wrath, their imposture, and their malice. Then *Moses* spoke thus; "O Earth take them." Immediately the Earth swallowed them three up to the Waste. *Moses* said again, "O Earth take them;" and the Earth took them in up to the Neck. Then *Caron* and his two Companions began to entreat *Moses* to be merciful to them; but *Moses* made no account of their Prayers, for he was too much incensed. On the contrary he pronounced the third time the same words, "O Earth take them, and detain them in thy Bowels till the day of Judgment."

Then the Earth swallow'd them up quite, and closed over their Heads. Then said God to *Moses:* "O *Moses,* thou art very inhumane, my Creatures implored thy mercy several times, and thou hast not had compassion on them. By my greatness, and by my glory, had they but once called upon me, they should have found me favourable, and ready to hear them."

After that (said the Author) those of the Children of *Israel* who were not wise, began to say; "*Moses* has not made imprecations against *Caron*, but to possess himself after his death of his Treasures, and his House."

Moses hearing of this was angry at it, and prayed to God that the House of *Caron* and all his goods might be swallowed into the bottom of the Earth. The All-mighty and All-good God testifies it himself, when he speaks thus; *"And we have made him and his House to descend into the Bowels of the Earth;"* he means Caron: and *"no man can relieve him against God, and he was not of those who are relieved."*

They relate that the Commander of the Faithful, *Omar* (Gods peace be with him) writ a Letter to *Gamrou,* the son of *Gasus,* who commanded in *Egypt,* after he

Omars Letter to *Gamrou.*

had Conquered it, and had disposed of the affairs thereof, and had imposed the Tribute on such as he had received by composition, as well the *Coptites,* as the other Inhabitants of it. Behold the Tenure of that Letter:

"From *Gabdol Omar,* the son of *Chettab,* to *Gamrou* the son of *Gasus,* God give you his peace, O *Gamrou,* and his mercy, and his benedictions, and to all the *Mussulmans* generally. After that, I give God thanks for the favours he hath done you; there is no other God but he, and I pray him to bless *Mahumet* and his Family. I know, O *Gamrou,* by by the relation which hath been made me thereof, that the Province whereof you have the Government, is pleasant and well Fortify'd, well Cultivated, and very Populous; that the *Pharaos* and the *Amalekites* have Reigned there, that they have display'd therein the marks of their greatness, and of their pride, imagining they were Eternal, and taking where they had not made any accompt. But now God hath established you in their Habitations, and put into your power their Wealth, their Servants, and their Children, and made you Inheritor of their Land; praise, and blessing, and thanks be to him. To him belongs honour and glory. When you have received this my Letter, write me the particular qualities of *Egypt,* as well in respect of the Land as the Sea, and make me know it as if I had seen it my self. God preserve you."

Gamrou having received this Letter, and seen what it contained, answered *Omar,* (Gods peace be with him) and writ to him in these terms:

Gamrou's answer to Omar.

"From *Gabdol Gamrou,* the son of *Gasus,* the Son of *Vail,* the *Saamian,* to the Successor of the Apostle of God, (Gods peace and mercy be with him) *Omar* the son of *Chettab,* Commander of the Faithful, one of the *Chaliphs* according to the right way, whose Letter I have received and read, and understood his intention; wherefore I will dispel from his spirit the cloud of uncertainty, by the truth of my discourse. From God comes strength and power, and all things return to him. Know Lord Commander of the Faithful, that the Countrey of *Egypt* is nothing but a blackish Soil, and green Plants between a dusty Mountain and a reddish Sand. Between its Mountain and its Sand there are high-raised Plains, and levelled Eminences. It is surrounded by an Ascent which supplies it with provisions, and is in compass from *Syene* to the extremities of the Land, and the side of the Sea, a Moneths riding for a Man on Horse-back. Through the midst of the Countrey there runs a River, blest in the morning, and favoured of Heaven at night, which rises and falls according to the course of the Sun and Moon. It hath its time, wherein the Springs and Sources of the Earth are opened to it, according to the command given them by its Creator, who governs and dispenses its course, to supply the Province with sustenance; and it follows according to the order prescribed it, till such time as its waters being risen, and its Waves rolling with noise, and its surges being come to their greatest elevation, the Inhabitants of the Countrey cannot pass from one Village to another, but in little Boats, and a man sees the little Wherryes turning to and fro, as white and black Camels in the imaginations of the people. Then when it is come to this condition. behold it begins to return back, and to confine it self within its Chanels, as it came out of it before, and rose up by little and little. And then the most forward, and the most slothful prepare themselves for labour, they are scattered up and down the Fields in multitudes, the people of the Law, whom God preserve, and the people of Alliance, whom men protect; they are seen stirring to and fro like Ants, some weak, others strong, and wearying themselves out at the task imposed upon them; for that is not obtained of them by their good will, but by force and constraint, by ill-treating and oppressing them. They are seen searching into the Earth, and turning up so much of it as hath been overflown, and casting into it all sorts of Grain, which they hope (with the assistance of God) will multiply therein. And it will not be long ere the Earth puts off the black hew of its manure, and cloaths it self in green, and casts forth a pleasant scent; while it produces Stalks, and Leaves, and Ears, making a delightful show, and giving a good hope, the dew of Heaven watering it from above, and the moisture giving nourishment to its productions from beneath. Sometime there come certain Clouds, with a little Rain, sometimes there fall onely certain drops of water, and sometimes none at all. After that, Lord Commander of the Faithful, the Earth displays her Beauties, and makes a Triumph of her Favours, cheering up the Inhabitants, and assuring them of a good Harvest of her Fruits, for the sustenance of them and their Cattel, and to be Transported elsewhere, and to make their Beasts multiply. She appears now (Lord Commander of the Faithful) like dusty ground, then presently it is a blewish Sea, and as it were a white Pearl, then like black Dirt, then as green Taffata, then as a piece of Embrodery of divers colours, then like a fount of molten Gold. Then they Harvest their Corn, which being Thrash'd out passes afterward diversly among Men, some taking what belongs to them, and others what does not belong to them. This vicissitude returns every year, every thing in its Season, according to the order and providence of the All-mighty; may that great God be ever praised, blessed be he, the best of Creatures. As to what is necessary for the carrying on of these Works, and what should make the Countrey populous, and well cultivated, maintain it in a good condition, and make it advance from good to better, according to what hath been told us by such as are acquainted therewith, as having had the government of it in their hands, we have made a particular observation of three things; The first is, not to credit the malicious discourses of the meaner sort of people, against the chiefest of the Countrey, because they are envious, and unthankful for the good which is done them. The second is, to lay out one third of the Tribute raised therein towards the reparation of Bridges, and

Causeys. And the third is, not to raise the Tribute out of any Species, till it be in its perfection. This is the Description of *Egypt*, Lord Commander of the Faithful, whereby you may know it, as if you had seen it your self. God continue you in your good conduct, and make you happily manage your Empire, and assist you to undergo the charge he hath imposed on you, and inspire you with an acknowledgment of the favours he hath done you. Peace be with you; May God be praised, and assist with his favours and benedictions our Lord *Mahumet*, and those of his House, and those of his party."

The Commander of the Faithful *Omar* (Gods mercy on him) having read (says the Author) *Gamrou*'s Letter, spoke thus; "He hath made an exquisite Description of the Land of *Egypt* and its Appurtenances; he hath design'd it so well, that it cannot be mistaken by such as are capable of knowing things. Praised be God, O Assembly of *Mussulmans*, for the favours he hath done you, by bringing you into the possession of *Egypt*, and other Countries. He it is whose assistance we all ought to implore."

They relate, that when the House of *Gamrou*, the son of *Gasus*, was demolish'd and made part of the great Mosquey of *Masre*, there was found in a corner a stone, on which these verses were written: *"Slight not a favourable occasion, wherein thou maist stretch forth thy hand to do some good; We live but to die, and death is deceitfull; from one hour to another, there is a change of affairs."* They relate also that while the same *Gamrou* was Governour of *Egypt* certain *Coptites* came, and made evil reports to him against certain persons, about affairs which he knew nothing of, thinking by that means to insinuate themselves into his favour, and be powerful about him; but he reproved them of it saying; "O ye *Coptites*, who are here assembled, know that when any one comes to give us evil reports of his Brother, we shall advance his Brother to higher Dignity, and debase the Detractor, for the Detractor envies the prosperity of his Neighbour, and endeavours to ruine him; the cauldrons of his malice boil in his breast, so that it rises up into his Tongue, and these wicked discourses are the smoke of that fire which sets them a boyling. He said also

(Gods peace be with him) he who makes ill reports to thee, calumniates thy self; he who speaks ill to thee of another, speaks ill of thy self."

He said sometimes to his Captains, and those whom he employed about his affairs; "Use me not as a Dagger to stab people withall. Shew your selves kind and obliging to all, for who would live in peace must practise it. Be carefull to secure the High-ways, and protect Travellers; Punish the wicked, that they may be kept in by fear, and that the Marchant be in safety; Strive not with the weak for the things whereof they are possessed; claim not the thing wherewith they sustain themselves; eat not of their Bread in their Houses, that you may have no remorse of Conscience. Understand you not what is read to you out of the Book of your Lord, which was inspired into the heart of your Prophet? (Gods peace and mercy be with him.) He will not desire your goods of you, that you might not mutually desire them one of another, and that you be not covetous in your hearts, and that that may not make a discovery of your maliciousness."

Abunasre of the West (Gods mercy on him) in the Book of the Histories of *Egypt*, which God continue populous and well cultivated, says, that on the Castle-gate at *Masre*, in the time of the *Romans*, before the *Mussulmans* conquered *Egypt*, there was near the great Gate of the Church of *Mugalleca*, called the *Gate of Grace*, an Idol of Brass, in the form of a Camel, with the Figure of a man riding on him, having an *Arabian* Turbant on his Head, and his Bow over his Shoulder, and Shoes on his Feet.

A supposed Statue of *Mahumet* at *Masre*.

The *Romans* and the *Coptites*, when any one injured or unjustly persecuted another, came to that Statue, and standing before it, he who suffered the injury said to him who did it; "Give me what belongs to me, otherwise I will make my complaint to that Cavalier, who will oblige thee to do me right by fair means or by foul."

By that Cavalier they meant *Mahumet*, (Gods peace and mercy be with him) for it is written among them in the Law of *Moses* and the Gospel, where the countenance and posture of *Mahumet* is described; "He *shall ride on the Camel, and have Shoes on; he shall carry the* Arabian *Bow, and have a Turban on his Head*": Gods peace and mercy be with him. When *Gamrou* came to *Egypt* to conquer it, he and the *Mussulmans* (Gods peace be with them) the *Romans* perceiving they would certainly be subdued, and not doubting of the Victory of the *Mussulmans,* hid that Statue under ground, that it might not serve the *Mussulmans* for an Argument against them in the dispute. "I have heard (says the son of *Lahigus)* that that Statue had continued in that place several thousands of years, and that they knew not who had made it; God knows how it stands. This story minds me of another, which is this; The Sultan the *Malcolcamel, Mahumet* the son of *Abubeker,* the son of *Job* (Gods mercy on him) sent the son of *Sagad* Ambassador into one of the Islands of *Andalouzia,* the Soveraign whereof (as I think) was the Emperour. This Ambassador returning, related to the Sultan what strange things he had seen in the Island. He told him among other things he had seen, opposite to a Church belonging to the *Romans,* a Statue of Stone in the form of an Ass, with a man upon it, set on a square Pedestal, so that the Statue and the Pedestal were all of a piece, of a black bright stone; and all who entered into the Church, or came out of it, did spit upon the Statue, and railed at it, then turned away from it. I ask'd the King (continued the *Sagadian* as he related this story) as I sate with him, what figure that was, and he told me that the *Romans* thought it a Statue of the Prince of the *Mussulmans.* Whereupon (added he) I felt my self smitten with the Zeal of the *Mussulman* Religion, which obliged me to speak thus to him; 'Certainly great King, this people is ill informed of that Statue, and the opinion they have of it far from any likelihood of truth.' 'Why?' said the King. 'Because (said I) he whom they imagine it represent, never rid but upon Camels; on the contrary, 'tis the *Messias* (Gods peace be with him) who rode on an Ass.' The King thereupon sent for a company of Priests and Monks, and related my discours to them, and they doubted not but that I had reason, and spoke the truth, which made them presently consider what they should do with that Figure. The

Another alleged Statue of *Mahumet.*

result was, that ere next day was over, they prepared it a Chappel, where they lodg'd it in the Church, afterwards burning incense before it, and cloathing it with Silk, and making a Procession about it, and doing it great honours with much Devotion. 'This was a business (said they) which was concealed from us. This Figure had not been set up in this Countrey, had it not been the Figure of the *Messias;* for this is not the Countrey of the *Mussulmans,* and their Prince never came thither.'"

He who related this story, said to the Sultan; "Have I sinned in doing so?" "No, by the true God," said the Sultan, "on the the contrary, you have done well, and deserved reward; since what you did was out of the good zeal you had for the *Mussulman* Religion, and the service of the Prophet, Gods peace and mercy be with him." As to the Statue, that is it which the Christians adore, and wherein they put their hope.

The *Sangian* relates in his ancient Annals, that one of the *Caliphs* of this Province caused Tribute to be paid at great *Constantinople,* and that *Geuhar* General of the Armies of *Mugazzoldinil* built the City of *Cairo,* which was called from the name of the *Chaliph, Cairo* of the *Mugazzoldinil,* and founded the Castles. They say he dilated his Conquests as far as *Damas,* before the *Mugazzoldinil* entered into *Egypt.*

They relate, that in the seventh year of the Prophet's Retreat, God replenish him with his Favours and Benedictions, *Chatteb* the son of *Abubalig* came into *Egypt* from the *Mucaux,* bringing along with him Mary the Egyptian, and another young Lady, which they

Mary of Egypt.

said was her Sister, and that the Apostle of God (Gods peace and mercy be with him) bestow'd her on *Chasan* the son of *Thabet,* who had by her his son *Gabdorrachaman.* His Mule was a great Hedghog, and his Ass a wild Goat. The *Mucaux,* who was then *Cesar*'s Lieutenant in *Egypt,* made him a present of all that.

Gabdolaglai the *Othmanidan* relates what follows; "I said one day to the son of *Sagad,* the *Egyptian* Lawyer, (Gods mercy on him) 'Tell us something, whereby we may know the excellency of the Countrey of *Egypt.*' 'To that purpose (said he) 'twere sufficient to tell what Historians relate of the son of *Masgud,* and what the Prophet (Gods peace and mercy be with him) said to him of *Egypt* before he died. "We were together (said the son of *Masgud)* in the House of our Mother *Gaisa,* (Gods peace be with him) and the Apostle of God (Gods peace and mercy be with him) cast his eye on us, being pressed with pain, with tears in his eyes, and declared to us, that he should die within a short time, speaking to us in these terms; 'You are welcome, God give you a good and a long life, God preserve you, God govern you, God unite you, God protect you, God make you prosper, God raise you to honour, God give you peace. I recommend to you the fear of God, and I recommend you to the All-mighty and All-good God, and I pray him to have a care of you, after me.' 'O Apostle of God (said we to him,) when will your day be?' 'The time is very neer, (said he) behold I return to God, and to the Garden of Retirement, and the Paradise above.' 'Who shall wash you (said we) O Apostle of God?' 'The men of my House (reply'd he) according to the order of their nearness.' 'In what shall we bury you, O Apostle of God? (said we.)' 'In my Garments, if you please, (said he) or in those of the happy *Arabia,* or in the white ones of *Egypt.*' 'Who shall make the Prayer for you, O Apostle of God?' (said we weeping.) 'Trouble not your selves for that; (said he) God be merciful to you, and reward you for the care you have of your Prophet. When you have wash'd me, and laid me into a Sheet, put me into my Coffin, which is here by the side of my Tomb, then depart from me for a while, till my good friend *Gabriel* hath Prayed for me, and after him *Michael,* then *Esraphiel,* then the *Angel of Death,* with many other Angels, whom God Bless; After that return to me, and come near me one after another, and pray God heartily to grant me peace and mercy; and forbear importuning me with Cries, Weeping, and Lamentations. The first who shall make the Prayer for me, shall be the men of my own House, then their Wives, then you. Continue in peace with those of my Companions who are at a great distance from me; and with those who have followed me in my Religion, till the day of the Resurrection. I make you witnesses of the Benediction

The last words of Mahumet.

which I give all those who have embraced the *Mussulman* Religion.'" This is the Testament which the Prophet (God grant him peace and mercy) made before his death. It suffices for the glory of *Egypt*, that he mention'd it at his death, and that he ordered they should bury him in the white Garments of *Egypt*. What greater glory can there be then that!'"

Other words of Mahumet.

The incomparable old Man, Doctor of the sayings and actions of the Prophet *Abugabdol Mahumet*, the son of *Negaman* (Gods peace be with him) relates, upon the credit of him from whom he heard it, that the Apostle of God (God grant him peace and mercy) spoke one day in these terms; "The hand of God is upon *Egypt*, the Inhabitants of it are favoured with a particular Protection from God, and with a happy prosperity." The Ancient *Abugabdol* explicating these words of the Prophet, speaks thus; "That hand signifies Power and Divine assistance."

The words of a Sage of *Egypt*.

Guebad the son of *Mahumet*, (Gods peace be with him) speaks thus; "Sitting one day in the great Ancient Mosquery of *Masre*, which God preserve, I heard a Citizen who related it as a thing which he had learnt from some great Person, that it was on a time asked one of the Sages of *Egypt*, 'What is the most delightful thing that ever you saw?' 'Fruit (reply'd he) when they appear clustered all about the Trees and Plants like Clouds, which closely follow one another.' 'What was the best thing you did ever eat?' 'What was presented to me (said he) in a quiet place, without trouble and disturbance, when I have been very hungry.' 'What was the most pleasant Drink you ever tasted?' 'The remainders (said he) of the overflowing of the *Nile* of *Egypt* in the Spring time.' 'What was the most delightful thing you ever heard?' 'The eloquent voice (said he) of a Person reading the *Alcoran*, and pronouncing it distinctly, without Singing and without Artifice.' 'In what did you find your self most commodiously clad?' 'In Linnen half worn out (reply'd he) in Summer, and in any other Cloath or Stuffe in Winter.' 'Do you find any thing better then that?' 'Yes (reply'd he) Health.'"

The Prophets and devout Persons liv'd by their Labour.

It is related of one of Lawyers of *Egypt* (God shew him mercy) that he said; "I have heard a man who related in the Tent of the Commander of the Faithful *Gamrou* the son of *Gasus* (Gods peace be with him) or over against it, as a thing which he had from *Mecdad* the son of *Magdaquerbe*, the *Zebidian,* that the Prophet (Gods peace and mercy be with him) spoke thus; 'No man can eat any thing better in this World then what he eats by the labour of his hands. For the Prophet of God *David* liv'd by the labour of his hands.'"

'Tis related of *Bara* (Gods peace be with him) that he said thus upon this occasion; "The Prophets and Devout persons, have always endeavoured to get their Livelihood by lawful ways; *Adam* (Gods peace be with him) was a Labourer, *Seth* a Weaver, *Edrisus* a Taylor, *Noah* a Carpenter, *Cadar* a Mule-keeper, *David* an Armourer, *Abraham* a Sower of Seeds, others say a Weaver of Lawn, *Salich* a Marchant, *Moses* and *Saguib,* and *Mahumet,* (Gods peace and mercy be with them) were Shepherds, *Locman* a Taylor, *Jesus* the son of *Mary* a Pilgrim, *Abubeker,* and *Omar,* and *Othman,* and *Gali,* and *Gabdorrachaman,* the son of *Guph,* and *Talche,* were Merchants Trading in Cypres and Lawnes, *Maimoune* the son of *Meharam,* and *Mahumet* the son of *Sirin,* were also Lawn-Merchants, *Zebir* the son of *Gauam,* and *Gamrou* the son of *Gasus,* and *Gamer* the son of *Carir* were Silk-Merchants, *Job* the Skinner sold Goats-Skins, *Sagad* the son of *Abuvacas* drove a Trade in Dyers Woad, *Othman* the son of *Mahumet* the *Lachamian* was a Taylor, *Malich* the son of *Dinar* was a Writer."

The cries of a Devote at the Mosquey Gate of *Masre*.

Neguim the Deaf (God grant him mercy) related to me what follows; "There was (said he) in the *Caraph* at *Masre* a devout man, who stood every Friday at the Gate of the great old Mosquey, of the same side with *Gamrou*'s House, after the Prelate had concluded the Prayer, and cry'd out with a loud voice; '*There is no other God but the great God alone, without Associate; It is he who Reings; He ought to be Praised; Life and Death proceed from him; He ever lives and never dies; That which is good is in his Hand; To him all things return; He is able to do all things.*' All those who heard him repeated what he said, till there remained but few persons in the Mosquey; then at last he said; '*O Assembly of the Faithful, he who abstains from things forbidden, obtains remission of his Sins; he who is content with what God sends him, hath Wealth enough; he who eschews evil, is in safety.*' He ceased not to do this, till God call'd him, God grant him mercy. He lies Buried in the Cemitery of *Masre,* which God protect against its Enemies, and keep in his Holy custody, *Amen.*"

It is in God we hope, it is good to wait upon him; God grant peace to our Lord *Mahumet,* and to those of his House, and those of his Party, and fill him with his Benedictions. Behold the Book finish'd by the grace of our glorious Lord; let him be praised, and exalted, and glorify'd.

This Copy (which God Bless) was finished in Writing, the 14th. day of the venerable Moneth *Regebe,* in the year 992. at *Tibe* the Noble, God bless her Nobility, and replenish her with his Favours.

Tibe *is a City in* Arabia, *according to the* Geuharian. *The 14th. of* Regebe 992. *corresponds to the 22. of* July 1584.

FINIS.

APPENDIX

An Early Arabic Account of Pyramid Legends

Murtaḍā ibn al-'Afīf drew upon older sources in the compilation of his *Prodigies of Egypt*, many with roots dating back centuries. Among the most important of these versions is that of the *Akhbār al-zamān*, a text attrubited in the medieval period to the historian al-Mas'udi but today no longer believed to be his work. The text dates from somewhere between 904 and 1140 CE. The following excerpts from Book Two cover antediluvian pyramid legends that also appear in the work of Murtaḍā.

Chapter 1

... The first to build pyramids was Sūrīd, son of Sahlūq, who ruled Egypt three hundred years before the Flood. This king had a dream in which he felt as if the earth were overturned with all its inhabitants, the men fled in all directions, and the stars fell and clashed against each other with a terrible noise. He was moved by this dream and conceived a great fear; he nevertheless imparted his foreknowledge to no person, but he knew that some terrible event would happen in the world. Then he dreamed that the fixed stars descended on the earth in the form of white birds; these birds caught men in flight, and threw them between two high mountains which then closed over them; then the stars darkened and were eclipsed. This dream renewed his terrors. He entered the Temple of the Sun and began to pray and worship God in the dust, and wept. When morning came, he ordered the chief priests to come together from all parts of Egypt. One hundred and thirty of them met, and he secretly consulted with them on the visions he had seen. The priests praised him and glorified him, and they explained to him that a great event would occur in the world. Philemon, the high priest, spoke. He was their leader, and he lived constantly in the presence of the king; he was the priest of Ochmoun,* a city of ancient Egypt. He said: "No doubt the vision of a king is a wonder because the dreams of royal personages can be neither in vain nor misleading because of the greatness of their power and elevation of their rank. Allow me to share the king a dream that I had one year, which to date I have reported to no one." The king said, "Explain it to me, O Philemon." "I dreamed," he said, "that I sat with the king at the top of the lighthouse in Ochmoun; the sky lowered down close enough to touch our heads, and it formed over us a dome that enveloped us. The king raised his hands toward heaven, and the stars came down to us in a multitude of different forms. Men implored the help of the king and gathered around his palace. The king raised his hands up to his face, and he ordered me to do the same; and both of us were in great distress. Then we saw a kind of opening in the sky from which came a light, and we saw that light rise above us—it was the sun. We saw him and implored him, and he spoke to us, telling us that the heavens would return to their starting point after three hundred and sixty orbits had been made. The sky descended almost to touch the ground and then returned to its proper place. Then I awoke, filled with terror." The king commanded the priests to measure the altitude of the stars, and analyze what they portended. They made the calculations with great care, and they spoke first of a flood and then of a fire, which would burn the entire world. Then the king ordered the construction of the pyramids, and when they were completed according to his wise plan, he transported to them the wonders and treasures of his people and the bodies of ancient kings. He ordered the priests to deposit therein the secrets of their science and precepts of their wisdom. But the most famous of the descendants of Ham, the Copts and Indians, are the wise.

---

* The author has inadvertently for substituted Ochmoun for the ancient capital of Amsūs (Memphis).

Chapter 2

... Sūrīd sat on the throne of his father. He walked in the footsteps of Sahluq in justice and fairness, attended to the development of the culture of the land, ruled his subjects with gentleness, and even shared with them his assets and those of his relatives. He was the first to establish a property tax in Egypt, and to impose one on artisans within their means; the first also who ordered welfare for the sick and infirm at the expense of the treasury. He built lighthouses, erected monuments, and fashioned talismans and temples. During his reign the empire saw the greatest prosperity it had ever experienced. The people loved him and showered him with praise.

He built a mirror of a compound substance in which he saw the climates of the world with their inhabited parts and deserted parts and everything that happened in them. This mirror was placed in a copper lighthouse in the middle of the city of Amsus. The Copts say that it was fashioned primarily in Misr. It showed all the travelers who came to Egypt from all directions, and they therefore could take precautions against them. This king was also the first who kept records, in which he wrote every day about what had happened and what he had done; he placed these sheets in his library, and at the end of each month he carried them to the treasury, with the papers of the ancient kings, after having affixed his seal. He extracted what was best in this record and had it engraved on stone. He even collected the masterpieces that were executed in his time, the marvels that were produced there; and he rewarded by generous donations that makers of these masterpieces.

In the middle of the capital he erected a statue of a woman sitting and holding a child to her breast as though to breastfeed. Any woman who had disease afflicting a part of her body could touch the corresponding portion of the body of the statue, and the malady would cease; so if her milk were to decline, she touched the statue's breasts and it would increase; if she wanted to curry favor with her husband, she touched the statue's face with fragrant grease, saying, "Get me this or that." If a woman had a sick child, she did the same with the child of the statue, and it was healed; if her children had a difficult character, she touched the child's head, and they grew sweeter. Young women also found relief, and if an adulterous woman were to put her hand on the statue, she felt a disorder so deep that despite herself she confessed her crime.[*] For issues that concerned the night they visited the statue at night, and for issues that concerned the day, they visited during the day. This idol performed many wonders until the time of the Flood, when it was destroyed. However, we read in a Coptic book she was only erected after the Flood and that the Egyptians of that time went to visit it and made it into a cult. Its image is reproduced in all of Egypt's temples and painted in many colors. It is said that the creators of this idol were the disciples of Philemon the priest. It is they who also taught the Egyptians all their arts. We'll talk about them later in this book.

Sūrīd executed many more marvels, among them the idol called Bokras, which was composed of several substances used in medicine. This idol had the property of combatting various diseases and poisons. They knew by it which patients were likely to recover; these were treated and fed according to certain signs that appeared in the idol, and the patients returned to health. Often the treatment involved washing the part of the statue corresponding to the one in which the patient was suffering and making the patient drink the water that had been used for this ablution. This soon saw the malady end.

Sūrīd is the builder of the two pyramids that are attributed to Shaddād ibn 'Ād. The Copts deny that either the 'Ādites or the Amalekites ever invaded their country because they say the Egyptians could defend themselves with their magic against any who attacked them. Al-Harabiun[†] says the same. Abū Ma'shar reported this opinion in his *Book of Thousands*.

The reason Sūrīd built the pyramids was the vision that we have reported in its proper place. He sent for his priests and astronomers and told them how he saw the sphere had descended to him in the guise of a

---

[*] The French translator has obscured this line to avoid sexual language.
[†] Likely an error for al-Harrāniyūn, i.e. the Harrians or Sabians.

woman, how the land with all its inhabitants had been overturned, and how the sun had been eclipsed. They then foretold to him the Deluge with all its circumstances.

This fact is told in a history book which was transmitted to the Copts by two brothers and found in a tomb on the chest of one of the corpses. The Copts say that these two men were the descendants of an Egyptian from ancient Egypt who escaped the rising deluge with Noah in the ark. He had believed the prophet, and he took his two sons with him. It is said he was a son of Misrām, son of Ham; he was an eminent and highly educated person. It is written in the book that King Sūrīd built three cities in the Sa'id and placed there many wonders. Later we will have occasion to speak again of these two brothers.

Thus, we read in this book that Sūrīd, son of Sahluq, having had the aforementioned vision, shared it with Filemun, the chief priest, and ordered the priests to consult the stars, to determine which events threatened the greatest part of the world. They immediately began their observations; they studied the sky very carefully and discovered a prodigy coming down from heaven and up from the earth would consume almost all men: this prodigy was to be a great flood, after which nothing would remain. The king asked if this event would recur several times or if it should be finished once and for all. They observed more and replied that the human race with its empires and all things on earth would reappear as they were before. Then the king ordered the construction of temples and great monuments, for himself and his family, in order to safeguard their bodies and all their riches, which they would deposit within. He inscribed on the ceilings, on the roofs, on the walls, and on columns, all the secrets of science, in which the Egyptians excelled more than any other nation; and he had painted a picture of the great stars and lesser stars, with signs that permitted their recognition. He also engraved the names of plants and their properties, how to construct talismans, their descriptions, and the rules of mathematics and geometry. All who know the books and the language of Egypt can make use of these images and inscriptions.

The priests told the king that when the following events took place, they would occur over the whole world except for a very small part, and the time of their realization would be when the heart of the Lion would be in the first minute of the head of Cancer, with the planets occupying the following positions: the moon in conjunction with the sun would be in the first minute of Aries; Zaus,[*] that is to say, Jupiter, would be at 29° of Pisces; Mars 28° 5′ of the same constellation; Aphrodite or Venus at 29° 3′; Hermes or Mercury at 27°; Saturn in Libra; and the apogee of the moon at 5° and a few minutes of Leo. The King, having heard the report, said to the priests, "Now look to see whether after this event there will come another from heaven onto the earth that will be the opposite of it, I mean to say, the destruction of the world by fire." They informed him that it would be so. "Look then," he said, "to see when this will happen." They resumed their observations and found that this deluge of fire would take place when the Heart of the Lion would be in the final minute of 10° of Leo; the Sun would be in the same minute in conjunction with Saturn and in trine compared to the Head; Mars would be in Leo in an oblique passage; and Mercury in the same minute as he; Siline[†] in Aquarius, in conjunction with the Tail, in twelve parts; Venus opposite her on a straight path; and Mars in Leo on a straight path. At that moment the sun will cover the earth in a manner heretofore unknown. The priests brought all this to the king and said: "When the Heart of the Lion will have completed two thirds of a revolution, there will be no living animal on earth that will not be stricken and die, and when it will have completed a full revolution, the system of the spheres will be destroyed."

The king ordered the construction of tall monuments, the cleaving of huge slabs, the extraction of lead from the land of the West, and the rolling in of stones from the region of Aswan; these great black rocks were drawn on chariots. He laid the foundations of the three pyramids, Eastern, Western and Colored; the last of these was entirely made of white

---

[*] Transliterated in Arabic from the Greek "Zeus."
[†] Selene; i.e., the Moon in Greek.

and black colored stones. It is said that the builders had palm wood sheets covered in writing, and after having extracted every stone and having it cut, they placed over each stone one of these sheets; they then gave a blow to the stone, and it traveled far beyond the reach of sight. They came back close to it and did the same again until they had led it to its assigned place. Craftsmen then carved each slab so as to affix in the middle an iron rod; they placed over it another slab with a hole in its center, and the rod entered the hole. They then poured lead around the slab and into the hole so that the adjustment was perfect.

They decorated the pyramids with paintings, inscriptions, and figures capable of confounding the imagination. The doors were placed forty cubits underground, in subterranean passages made of lead and stone; the length of each underground passage was one hundred fifty cubits. The door of the eastern pyramid was on its east side, a distance of one hundred cubits from the middle of the face. The door of the western pyramid was on its west side, also at the distance of one hundred cubits from the middle of the face; it corresponded with the door of the subterranean passage. The door to the colored pyramid, in stones of two colors, was on its north side, one hundred cubits from the middle of its face; they dug until they reached the door of the corresponding subterranean passage and thus passed into the door of the pyramid. The height of each of the pyramids was a hundred royal cubits, equivalent to five hundred cubits today. The length of each side was a hundred cubits; the faces rose perpendicularly up to forty cubits, and they then bowed inward so as to form sharp edges which joined at the top. They began construction in a time of happiness; people gathered to see them and were amazed. When they were finished, they covered them in gaudy silk from top to bottom, and they declared a feast in their honor which all persons in the empire were required to attend.

Then the king commanded the construction of storehouses in stones of flint of various colors. He filled the western pyramid with emerald objects, images made with the substances of the stars, wonderful talismans, iron tools of outstanding quality, weapons that cannot rust, glass objects that can bend without breaking, all types of drugs (simple and compounded), deadly poisons, and a host of other things too numerous to describe. Into the eastern pyramid, he transported the idols of the stars, representations of the heavens, wonders built by his ancestors, incense to offer to the idols, books containing the history of ancient Egypt, an account of the lives of the kings and the dates of all the events that had transpired, still other books comprising a proclamation of all that would happen in Egypt until the end of time, with a description of the paths of the fixed stars and their influence at every moment. He also placed vessels containing drugs and other similar things. In the third pyramid, he deposited the bodies of the priests in black flint coffins, and with nearly every priest he placed books which recounted all that he had done and the story of his life. The priests were then ranked in order. The first order was that of the Nazarites, that is to say, the priests who had served the seven stars[*] for seven years each. The word *Nazir* signified, among them, one who had mastered the totality of science. The second class consisted of priests who had served six stars, the third those who had served five, and so on; and each of these seven orders had a name. The king placed the coffins of the priests down the sides of the pyramid according to their rank, and near their bodies he placed the books they had written on gold leaf in which they had recorded the past and the future and a record of the wonders performed by each of them. On the walls he placed idols who were seen to perform all of the various arts, arranging them according to their rank and power. He wrote a description of their operations, how to accomplish them, and the utility of what had been drawn. Through engravings and images, he described the nature of all things, the science of law and the laws of all the sciences. Then he filled the pyramids with the treasures of the stars, all of the gifts that had been offered to their idols, and the treasures of the priests; the amount of wealth simply cannot be calculated.

---

[*] That is to say, the planets: the sun, the moon, and the five visible planets.

Finally he assigned a guard to each pyramid. The guardian of the eastern pyramid was an idol striped white and black, with two open and flashing eyes. This idol was sitting on a throne and held a kind of spear. When a man looked at him, he uttered a terrible cry, which made him lose consciousness; he would fall to the ground unconscious and could no longer get up, dying on the spot. The guardian of the western pyramid was a striped flint idol: he was standing, held a kind of spear, and wore a snake on his head. If a man approached him, the snake would jump on him, entwine around his neck and choke him before returning to the head of the idol. The guardian of the colored pyramid was a small idol of an eagle standing on a pedestal. He attracted everyone who looked at him, and left them to die at his feet. When all these things had been established, King Sūrīd entrusted surveillance to the invisible spirits and offered them sacrifices, so they would turn down anyone who would want to approach without providing the agreed-upon offerings and without performing the established rites in their honor.

The Copts say that the pyramids bear a painted inscription in Arabic whose interpretation is this: "I, Sūrīd, the king, built these pyramids at such and such a time. I completed the building in six years. Let anyone who would come after me and believe himself a king as great as I destroy them in six years, for all know that it is easier to destroy than to build. I also covered the pyramids in silk: Let those who come after me cover them in turn." For a very long period these monuments remained intact. As for covering them in silk, no king could do so without overspending and without possessing true madness.

A tradition also has it that when al-Ma'mūn had entered Egypt and saw the pyramids, he wanted to destroy one to know what it contained. He was told, "You cannot." He replied, "At least we can open a breach." And they made the gap that we still see by charring stone with fire, dousing it with vinegar, hitting it with rams, and then removing the cuttings with iron stakes. He spent a considerable sum on this work. They then found that the thickness of the wall was about twenty cubits. When they had pierced the wall, they found on the other side of the hole a green vase containing gold coins, and the weight of each dinar was one of our ounces; there were a thousand of these dinars. The workers were amazed at this discovery and did not understand the meaning of it. They informed al-Ma'mūn and brought him the gold and the vase. Al-Ma'mūn appeared amazed at the sight of the gold, noting how it was pure, bright, and red; then he said, "Show me the accounting of what you have spent in making this breach." This was calculated, and they found it to be exactly the value of that gold, neither more nor less. And Ma'mūn and his court stood speechless that this expenditure could have been calculated so far in advance, and that they could know exactly the place where the breach would be made. These (ancient) men had truly reached a level of science that no other had done, and which we ourselves have not reached, neither we nor our fellow men. It is said that the vase in which the sum was found was made of emerald and that Ma'mūn had it carried to his treasury. This is one of the wonders he brought from Egypt.

Among the extraordinary facts of Egypt, the following is still quoted: After Ma'mūn had opened the breach in the pyramid, the workers continued to work for several years. They eventually penetrated it, and they went down along a slope that plunged into the monument. Some of them returned unharmed, but others perished. There are a host of traditions about it.

Twenty men agreed together to enter the pyramid and not to come out until they had reached the bottom, or died. They took with them food and drink for two months. They brought supplies to make fire with, candles, ropes, picks, and all the tools they might need. They entered the pyramid; they went down the first hallway and the second slope. Continuing to walk on the floor of the pyramid, they saw bats as big as eagles, which slapped at their faces. And then they came to an opening from which came a cold wind did not stop. They wanted to enter, but the wind extinguished their torches; they placed them in glass, and they returned to the opening to try to enter. Now they saw that the bottom of the hole was closed off by a great slab of a precious substance, and they understood that below were the bodies of kings, with their gold and treasures.

But they did not know how to get down there. One of them said, "Tie me with ropes, and lower me down this hole until I reached the slab. Maybe I'll find a way to raise it." They did as he asked; his companions tied him with ropes around the middle of his body and they lowered him down in the hole; he remained there for a long time, his companions still holding the ropes; but in the end the hole closed behind him. In vain did the others make every effort to reopen it, but they could no longer reach him. They heard his bones breaking, and a terrifying voice made them fall over in a faint. When they awakened, they sought to escape. This they managed with great difficulty, several of the men, having fallen when climbing the corridors, were abandoned by the rest and perished. Those who survived finally came out of the pyramids; as they sat together at the pyramids' feet, they saw rise up from the ground before them that one of their companions who had perished in the hole. He now seemed to be alive, and he spoke to them in a cryptic language, and said unto them words whose meaning they did not understand; but his words were explained to them later by a scholar of the Sa'id. They meant: "Such is the fate of one who covets treasures that are not for him." After uttering these words, the man stopped talking and fell back down dead. They took away his body. They were arrested as murder suspects and brought before the *wali*, and there they related what had happened to them.

One may read of another tradition that some men entered the pyramids, went down to the bottom, and made a turn. They saw a path like the one through which they came in, and they found therein a type of vase from which water dripped without decreasing; they did not understand what it was. Then they came to a place that resembled a square room whose walls were made of small square stones, colorful and magnificently beautiful. One of them took one of the stones he found and put it in his mouth, and immediately his ears were deafened by the wind. He had to endure this inconvenience the whole time he was in that company. These men then came to a place where they saw large piles of gold coins, struck with extreme perfection. The value of each piece was a thousand dinars. They took one, but they were no longer able to walk or move, and they were obliged to throw it back. In another place they saw a couch on which sat a sheikh made from green granite, wrapped in a cloak and having before him statues in the shape of small boys which it seemed like he was teaching. They took one, but they could no longer move. They returned whence they came, and from another closed room came a frightening buzzing and humming; they did not enter and went on by. They entered a square room where they saw a rooster made of precious stone, standing on a green pillar, and whose eyes lit up the whole room. As soon as they approached it, it uttered a terrible cry and flapped its wings, and they left it. They passed near a white stone idol, with the figure of a woman hanging upside down; at her side, two stone lions seemed to want to devour her. They fled and continued on their way. Having walked a long time, they reached a point where they saw ahead of them a ray of light; they followed it and they reached a gateway where they came out again onto the rocks; at the gate of the hole they noticed two statues of black stone armed with javelins. This surprised them. Then they walked up a slope, and after following it for a whole day, they returned from the pyramids to the outside. This occurred in the time when Abd Allah, son of Abd al-Malik, was governor of Egypt. These men came and told him of their adventure, and he sent someone to search with them for the hole through which they had come out; but they searched for several days at the same place without being able to find it, and to their surprise they discovered neither trail nor sign that could lead them there. He who published this story found a precious stone which he sold for a large sum.

It is said that the time of Ahmed, son of Tulun, men entered the pyramids and found in the arch of one of its rooms a glass jug, which they took and brought back. A man of their company lost his way; they went looking for him, but he came to meet them naked and giggling, and said, "Do not worry for me." Then he ran back to the entrance of the pyramid. They understood that a *djinn* had seized him. This adventure leaked out, or a man of the company betrayed his companions; the Sultan seized the jug and forbade anyone from entering the pyramids. The jug was weighed, and they found it contained seven *ratl* of white and clear glass.

A scholar stood up and said, "The ancient kings did nothing in vain, so this object must have a purpose." Then he filled it with water and weighed it again; he found that its weight remained exactly the same.

It is said that some men entered the pyramids with a young boy to use him for sex. They saw a black slave armed with a cane coming at them, and he began to give them terrible blows. They fled immediately, leaving behind their food, their drinks, and some of their clothes. The same thing happened, it is said, to other men in the temple at Akhmim.

A man and a woman entered the pyramid to have sex with each other; they were thrown to the ground and seized with a furious delirium that lasted until their death.

It is said in some books of the Copts that King Sūrīd, after hearing the priests tell him that a fire would come from beyond the sign of Leo and burn up the world, made underground passageways in the pyramids in preparation; the Nile could be brought into these underground passages and discharged from there at several points in the western territory and in the land of Sa'id. The King filled these channels with wonders, talismans, and idols.

Some Copts say that King Sūrīd, having heard the report of astronomers, said, "See if yet some other disaster will threaten this country." They made observations and said, "A deluge will threaten to submerge the majority of the country, which will be devastated for several years, after which its prosperity will be reborn." "What," asked the king, "will be the cause of this devastation?" They said, "A king will massacre his own people and take their wealth." "And then?" he asked. "The country's prosperity will be reborn from the murder of the king." "And then?" "Monstrous men will come along the side of the Nile will invade and occupy the greatest part of the land." "And then?" "They will cross the Nile, and they will take the people into captivity." Sūrīd ordered their predictions inscribed on the pyramids, on monuments, and on stones.

A man from the land of the West, one of those who make a business of going on camels to carry fish to the oasis, said he had to stay overnight at the pyramids; having heard a noise and a sort of gushing that never ceased, he was afraid and went away; he then saw around the pyramid shining lights, and these he observed for a long time, until he was overcome by sleep. The next morning when he awoke, he saw other fish beside his own fish; astonished, he put the fish that he had back on his camel, and he hastened to return to Fustat, while vowing never to return to the pyramids.

The temples also have many stories too numerous to relate. There are traditions among the Copts of guardian spirits of the temples and the pyramids. According to these traditions, the spirit of the southern pyramid has the form of a naked woman, very beautiful and whose hair is divided into two. When she wishes to seize a man, she laughs in his face, then draws him near to her. When he approaches, she grabs him and he loses his reason. Many people have seen this woman wandering around the pyramid at noon or at sunset. The spirit of the other pyramid is a beardless naked yellow boy whose hair is divided into two; he is often seen to walk in circles around the monument. The spirit of the colored pyramid is shaped like a sea-sheik carrying a basket and having in his hand a censer such as those used in churches. These traditions are in in all the collections.

The temple of Akhmim, according to the belief of the people, has for its spirit guardian a young boy, black and naked. The spirit of the temple of Semenud is a sheikh of dark complexion, with long hair and a short beard. The spirit of the temple of Kobt (Coptos) has the form of a black servant carrying a little black child. The spirit of temple of Dendera has the form of a man with a lion's head and two horns. The spirit of the temple of Busir has the form of a white sheikh, dressed as a monk and carrying a book. The spirit of the temple of the 'Ādites has the form of a shepherd equipped with a stick. The Dahshur pyramids have spirits that can see when anyone approaches from any side whatsoever and any time of day. There is, for each of these monuments, certain offerings and some incenses that allow access to their treasures, and agreements can be made between their spirits and men.

Sūrīd reigned one hundred and seven years. The priests had made known to him in advance the time of his death. He bequeathed power to his son Hardjit with all the lessons he would need, and he ordered him to place his body in the pyramid, in the place he had prepared; he recommended that it be embalmed in camphor and they should place with him the valuable tools, arms, and instruments he had collected in advance. Hardjit executed all that his father had commanded of him, and he took in his hand the reins of power.

[...]

[Lastly,] Far'ân sat on the throne and donned the tiara. No one dared resist him, and all the people remained quiet under his government, because he had power and an extraordinary courage. He dominated the earth, and his heart was filled with pride. It was during his reign that the Flood arrived. He seized the property of his subjects, and he went further on the path of injustice than any man before him. He committed countless murders, and his courtiers followed his example. The princes dreaded him; they had to submit all his demands.

This is the Far'ân who wrote to Darmashil son of Yamhawîl, king of Babel, to ask him to destroy Noah. He sent messengers throughout all the lands of his empire to inquire about their gods and idols. He was told the story of Noah and he heard that the prophet wanted to wipe out from among the people the cult of idols, and he believed in a different God from them and an invisible one; it was also added that no one believed in his claims. When Noah was set to build the ark, Far'ân wanted to give the order to kill him and burn his ship. A vizier advised him not to do it because, he said, if the predictions of Noah should be true, the king might use the vessel with his household. This view was accepted, and king rescinded his order. However, he still thought to destroy Noah, but God stopped him. Knowledge of the Flood had spread among the Egyptians, but they did not know how high the waters would rise or how long they would stay on the surface of the earth. They built subterranean passages that they fitted with plated glass and within which they imprisoned the winds. The king took Philemon, the chief priest, with him that he might serve as protection for him and those of his household. He had, however, removed or exiled the priests.

One night Philemon had a dream in which he saw the city of Amsus overthrown with all its inhabitants, and idols threw their faces against the ground. Angels descended from heaven, armed with curved sticks with which they beat the men. Philemon said, "Why do you do this, and why do you have no pity for men?" They said, "It is because they have denied the God who created them." "And does he have for them any means of salvation?" They replied, "Yes. Whoever would be save should seek out the builder of the ark." Philemon awoke frightened and remained undecided and sad, uncertain what to do. He had a wife and two children, a boy and a girl, and seven disciples. Together, they resolved to go find Noah. Philemon, on yet another night, had a dream in which he thought he saw a verdant garden where white birds were flying and spreading the odor of musk. While he admired the beauty of the garden, the birds began to speak to him and said: "Go and assemble the believers." Philemon asked: "And who are these believers?" "They are," replied the bird, "the builders of the ark." The priest awoke, filled with confusion, and he told his vision to his parents and to his disciples, advising them to keep it secret. Then he set about reducing his possessions and selling the property he no longer needed; when he had finished the preparations in secret, he went to the king and said, "If the king wants to send me to Darmashil, I will see the man who is building the ark. I will observe and I will discuss with him this new religion that he claims to reveal to men. Therefore, I shall recognize whether his mission is real; but it is more likely that my visit will be the cause of its forfeiture and will show the futility of his claims." The king, delighted with this speech, gave Philemon the order to leave. He handed him a letter for Darmashil. The priest left with his family and with his disciples, and ventured into the land of Babel. There he went to Noah and told him why he had come; then he asked him to explain his doctrine. Noah satisfied his desire, and Philemon believed in him and all his companions. Philemon did not go to Darmashil, nor did he give him the letter from Far'ân, and he did not even see it. Noah said: "When God wants something good for a man, nothing can stop his desire to accomplish it." Philemon stayed with Noah, busy serving him with his children and his followers, until they went up together into the ark.

Far'ân continued to walk in the way of error and injustice, consumed in pleasures. He abandoned the temples, let wither the fruits of the soil, increased injustice, and grew the number of murders. Cultivation was abandoned, and the land everywhere became barren; men committed outrages upon each other and felt no remorse. The temples and *birba** were closed, their doors bricked shut. Finally the flood came, and the rain fell on Egypt for twenty-four days. Far'ân, constantly intoxicated, did not budge until the water had risen quite high; he stood up in haste to reach the pyramids. But the earth shook under him. He returned, looking for the subterranean passages, but he lost his footing and fell on his face onto the ground. He let out moans similar to those of a bull and was finally overwhelmed by the Flood. Those of his companions who penetrated into the subterranean passages were drowned. The water reached a quarter of the way up the pyramids; its mark is still visible today.

They say that some places were free from the Flood. This is the opinion of the Persians, who claim not to have known the Flood, and the Indians, who say the same for them. But all historians agree in affirming that the Flood spread universally over the earth.

---

* Great temples, from a Coptic word for ancient Egyptian temples.

Made in the USA
Monee, IL
19 September 2023